IT DEPENDS

A Guide to Peace Corps

WRITTEN BY KELLY BRANYIK

It Depends: A Guide to Peace Corps by Kelly Branyik

www.writewithlightpublications.com

Published by Write With Light Publications LLC Colorado
Cover Design by Colton Davies of coltondavies.com, Montana
Edited by Write With Light Publications LLC

Library of Congress Control Number: 2017908370
ISBN: 0-9802366-7-3

Second Edition

Printed in the United States of America

CONTENTS

ACKNOWLEDGMENTS

THERE ARE MANY I would like to express my gratitude for when it comes to this book. I believe we are our own most excellent motivator, but I also believe we're even stronger when our loved ones are by our side and supporting us. We never truly accomplish things alone.

THANK YOU to God for blessing me with many gifts, talents, and life experiences. My family for supporting me and helping me be the "light." To the China 20s for being my inspiration and helping me see the world with new eyes. To Dr. Donna Souder for exposing me to travel and sparking the adventure in me. Sandy Peng for following her intuition and having faith I could do this. To my colleagues and friends Erin Hu, Anne Zhang, and June Ji. Mama, Baba, and Soe for taking me in and loving me like family. Write With Light Publications LLC for their assistance in making this real.

AND the Returned Peace Corps Volunteers (RPCVs) who contributed their incredible, and real stories to this book. You dedicated a great of heartfelt content for the sake of this book, and I am forever grateful.

Brian Fassett
Danielle J. Zemmel
Jacqueline Gerson
Jenna Smith
John Gallo
Judson L. Moore
Natalie Ziemba

Thank you all so much for helping me make this dream a reality.

THE THREE PEACE CORPS GOALS & GLOSSARY OF TERMS

PEACE CORPS GOALS

As an organization, Peace Corps created goals for the volunteers to carry out during their service and after service completion. Below are the three primary goals of a Peace Corps Volunteer.

1. To help the people of interested countries in meeting their need for trained men and women.
2. To help promote a better understanding of Americans on the part of the peoples served.
3. To help promote a better understanding of other peoples on the part of Americans.

GLOSSARY OF PEACE CORPS TERMS

The glossary of terms is a compilation of words you will read and learn to recognize throughout this book and come to understand as you go through service.

Peace Corps Trainee (PCT): Currently in training
Peace Corps Volunteer (PCV): Currently in service
Returned Peace Corps Volunteer (RPCV): Completed Service
Pre-Service Training (PST): 2 to 3 months training before service
In-Service Training (IST): Training during service
Host Country National (HCN): Person native to the country of service
Close of Service (COS): Training toward the end of service
Site: Where volunteer will live and serve
Site Mate: Partner volunteer who lives and serves nearby
Expat: Someone temporarily residing in a foreign country

CONSIDERING PEACE CORPS

THE TOUGHEST JOB I ever loved started as a mere consideration as I was finishing up my time as a college student in Pueblo, Colorado. Looking back, I was so young then. I was working on my third year at CSU-Pueblo, not knowing where I was going next. For three years, I had known college, was focused on that phase of my life, and hadn't thought about what would happen after.

A few years before I graduated, my favorite professor gave me an opportunity, one I almost passed up. CSU-Pueblo was offering a 6-week study abroad program with EF Tours through the English department that allowed a select group of college students to venture overseas. The cost was about $7,000 per student and took me to France and Spain. It was the first time I would experience international travel.

The word 'excitement' could not begin to cover how I felt when I was on the 9-hour flight from Denver to Paris. I peered out the window to see masses of the blue ocean below and white specks where cruise ships were. I imagined getting to Paris, eating lavender honey on croissants and sipping wine on the Seine. What I had expected was not what I got.

What I got instead was warm hot chocolate at Angelina's Cafe near the Louvre, I walked through the aqueduct at the Pont du Garde. I lost my breath at the sight of the St. Chapelle Cathedral's stained glass windows. I climbed the Eiffel Tower in the rain. I watched the sunset at the Montmartre. I wandered through Carcassonne, you get the idea.

I saw everything I could imagine and even more, and I fell in love with international travel and all I had seen.

We traveled to Paris, Nimes, Avignon, Figueres, Barcelona, and Madrid. What I experienced in that short 12-day period changed how I thought about the world. After that trip, I knew I needed to see more of the world. That's when I decided to pursue a career that would allow me to travel and be a writer at the same time.

After returning from France and Spain, I searched for options that could take me abroad and allow me to write about the places I had been, the things I had seen, and the people I met. And yet, I couldn't find a way to live my dream and survive in this world.

I was taking a Careers for English Majors Course in Spring 2013 and on the verge of graduating when I discovered my next path in a book. As the professor began her lecture, I got lost in the assigned textbook full of people's success stories. I read through individual's experiences going from college English major to significant corporate achievements, partners, or CEOs of companies. I was impressed by how each person transitioned from an English Degree to a career they loved. I read through a few stories before stopping on a page about a woman whose name I can't remember. In the first few lines of her story, she talked about her time with Peace Corps. I read through to the end then thought to myself, "Huh. Peace Corps."

I had always known that Peace Corps existed, but I never knew exactly what it was or what it entailed. I went to the Peace Corps website and read its contents. Within a few hours, I knew this was the next path for me. In that same day, I called my parents to tell them I was going to join Peace Corps and their reaction?

"Go for it."

The process of applying to Peace Corps started in March of 2013 and took 11 months to complete. During that time, I looked for all information I could find about what to expect from the application process and Peace Corps service. As I searched for answers and learned about people's experiences in Peace Corps, I felt there was little information was out there to answer my questions. This sparked my motivation to educate future volunteers on what to expect and thus began my blog.

The idea of leaving home was never an easy thing for me. Two days before my dad took me to Denver International Airport to leave for Peace Corps, I became ill. I was so nervous to leave behind my home and family that I made myself sick. Some would call this a "do or die" moment. Either you decide to do it now, or your heart dies later because you regret not having done it. At least that's how I saw it.

I'm sure at that point normal parents would've been hovering over me in the bathroom while my head was in the toilet using their 'parent voice' saying something like, "You don't have to do this if you don't want to." But my parents aren't normal (in a good way). They are the most supportive parents of all time and encouraged me to move forward and do what I promised I would.

I never called my parents into the dim bathroom lit only by a night light. I sat alone on the floor next to the toilet trying to keep my stomach intact. I was in the bathroom, by myself wondering how I could be this crazy and why this decision made me this nervous. Why hadn't I chosen something safer or closer to home? So, while vomiting, I went through and considered the benefits of my decision.

For me, finding my dream job wasn't easy for someone with an English Degree, or so I'd been told. Too many times had I heard people say, "Oh, English? Are you going to be a teacher?" I replied with an irritated 'no' and told them I wanted to be a successful travel writer someday. They looked at me questionably, and said, "Oh. That's nice. Well... Good luck with that."

Before I decided to join Peace Corps, I spent months applying for jobs and internships and all of them required two-years of experience, which I didn't have and couldn't get because no one was hiring unless you had experience. I also had a great need to travel and to write. I had little money and a lot of school debt. When I weighed my options against my current situation, Peace Corps was the clear and most sensible decision for me, and it had everything I wanted to do.

I had built up my anxiety for far too long. As my head was drooped over the toilet, I imagined some other American family on the other side of the country celebrating in a less vomitus way. The truth is, I didn't want to

3

worry my parents. They knew I was struggling with the subsequent separation and experiencing a new world.

The day before I left, I looked my parents in the eye and said, "If I am struggling and I call home talking something crazy about quitting Peace Corps, you tell me to suck it up."

Of all the people in the world who could've easily convinced me to come home, my parents honored my requests and supported me the whole way.

Two days after my nervous vomiting incident, my father drove me to Denver, we shared our last lunch together for a while, and then he dropped me off at the airport hotel with my whole life in three suitcases. I remember not crying. Leaving was so overwhelming that I couldn't.

The next morning, I hauled myself and three suitcases on board and flew to Los Angeles for Orientation. A day later, 83 PCTs hopped on an indirect flight to Chengdu, Sichuan, China, stopping in Thailand and Tokyo on the way.

Two years away from home is a significant commitment and a big challenge. I've noticed there are times people consider joining but then make excuses for why they can't commit.

Maybe they have financial struggles, maybe their family doesn't agree, perhaps they are in a long-term relationship, perhaps they have kids, maybe they are already married, perhaps they think they are too old, or perhaps they're just afraid they won't be able to do it. The reasons are endless. Just like we make excuses to not go on vacation or to not buy that thing we really want, we make excuses to not volunteer.

What if you didn't have these excuses, struggles, or ties to your home, family, and situations? Would you join Peace Corps? Have you already made the decision?

Consider how Peace Corps will benefit you in the long run and consider the ways you could grow.

"IT DEPENDS"
By now, you've read through the Peace Corps website and discovered the benefits of being a Peace Corps Volunteer. You know the first goal is "To help the people of interested countries in meeting their need for trained

men and women."

But Peace Corps doesn't rush to tell you everything it entails. And why don't they tell you? Because each experience is different depending on the country, the time, the volunteer, current events, and a multitude of other reasons.

In Peace Corps, you'll have a lot of questions about what to expect, and you will sit hopefully waiting for answers that will ease you. The Peace Corps staff will answer your questions with a simple and somewhat annoying phrase.

"It Depends," they will say. At first, this phrase was so aggravating because we wanted answers to the how and the what. It would truly depend on each of us because no one is the same or will have the same experience.

Subconsciously, we started making up our own expectations, ones you have probably already heard. They include and are not limited to:

- I'm going to help people
- I'm going to lose weight
- I'm going to become fluent in the language
- I'm going to change the world
- I'm going to be close to my community
- I'm going to meet the love of my life
- I'm going to travel a lot
- I'm going to make a difference

Maybe some of these are true, and many of them will most definitely be true. But it depends.

By joining Peace Corps, you will get all of Peace Corps' juicy government benefits which I will explain later. The benefits include Financial, Student Loan Help, Travel experience, Career Services, Medical and Dental Coverage, and Graduate School opportunities. Consider these fantastic benefits when making the big decision to join. These benefits are further explained at PeaceCorps.gov.

FINANCIAL BENEFITS
You will be living off a small monthly stipend during your service, which equals the same amount your average HCN would make. If you are looking for a decent salary, Peace Corps may not be your best option.

After completing your service, you get over $8,000 readjustment allowance, pre-tax, (this amount increases every few years or so). You can do what you want with this money once you have completed your service, save it, go on a big trip, pay off a loan, whatever your heart's desire.

STUDENT LOAN BENEFITS
You will get Student Loan assistance once your service is completed. And while in service, your student loans are deferred. Public Loan Forgiveness is offered to those who weren't blessed with the Perkins Loans. With Public Loan Forgiveness, I will be able to pay off the other half of my loans if I make payments on time, every month for the next ten years.

If you do have Perkins loans, you may be eligible for partial cancellation. Either way, both are significant benefits if you have a severe amount of student loan debt. Talking to your loan providers about your options is essential.

TRAVEL BENEFITS
Before I left for Peace Corps China, I made a list of 22 places I wanted to see in China. On the Peace Corps monthly allowance, I was able to visit half of those destinations during my two years. Although I didn't see all the places I expected to, I saw more than most people will ever see and I did it with a minimal budget. In the various countries Peace Corps serves in, there are endless routes for adventure. You just have to look for them.

One of your greatest benefits of travel is you'll evolve into a local. You'll know the hidden gems in your community and your country of service. As a volunteer, we have an advantage that tourists just don't have. Through research and word of mouth, you can find pick up soccer leagues just a few train stops from home, the best hiking spot in a remote area, or the tree with the best fruit. My favorite places in China were the places the tourist wouldn't visit or know about because they visited for a short time. During service, you are allotted two days off for every month, not including your weekends, and you can save them and use them all at once to travel somewhere fantastic. Travel time may vary depending on the country you live in.

MEDICAL AND DENTAL
During your Peace Corps service, you are entirely covered by the Peace Corps organization. You receive full medical and dental coverage, which can come in handy during situations when you bite down on metal

chopsticks trying to eat a steamed bun (totally happened).

If you have dental issues, need surgery or broke something valuable, Peace Corps will decide how to proceed with medical attention. You won't even need to open your wallet.

CAREER BENEFITS

Peace Corps now gives future volunteers the chance to choose their country of service, thus catering more to their needs and to their desired career paths. In lieu of that, Peace Corps offers excellent support for RPCVs once they have completed their service including Non-Competitive Eligibility (NCE), which gives you an advantage when applying for government work. The jobs are endless, and many have chosen their perfect professions in job areas from business to arts. It depends on the preferred route. And with Peace Corps on your resume, you'll have some flair.

GRADUATE BENEFITS

Stipends and student aid are offered to those who want to take a shot at graduate school. Many universities recognize RPCVs and their substantial efforts and are more than welcoming to those ready to pursue a graduate degree. Peace Corps used to have an option called Master's International, which allows you to join the Peace Corps experience and achieve your Master's degree at the same time. However, they do not provide this program anymore.

YOU WILL GROW

Being in Peace Corps, I experienced positive changes in myself that I know I wouldn't have experienced back home. I needed a change, and I needed an experience that would help me grow out of my old self. I developed, and I transformed very quickly during my time in Peace Corps. During PST, many recognized me as being "impatient," "immature," and "negative." Six months into my service, I had changed so drastically the PC China staff, my friends, and peers commented on the positive change in me. That was the last thing I ever expected to have.

China had humbled me and reminded me that I was a tiny piece in a huge world. China forced me to look at my worst flaws and my strengths. it gave me the opportunity to decide what kind of person I wanted to be and how I wanted to represent myself to the world. This was also something I didn't expect to happen.

Aside from myself, I have witnessed volunteers with blind bravery accomplish Peace Corps Service like this was just another side journey, and I have seen people go through significant challenges during their service. It's a real testament to how much of your service is unknown, unexpected, and unprecedented. I believe many of those people came out with a better understanding of themselves and the world. That, I believe, is something to consider when choosing Peace Corps as your next adventure.

Now that you're considering Peace Corps let's do an exercise below.

- What are you expecting out of Peace Corps?
- What do you hope to gain from your service?
- What will you do if Peace Corps is not what you expected?

Talking more about expectations, I want to lead into Brian's story and read another perspective on expectations for Peace Corps. It is absolutely alright if you have the expectations, but as a piece of advice from me, I recommend keeping a more open mind and letting things wash over you. Here is what Brian expected from his Peace Corps experience. One I think many of you who have joined or are still considering, can relate to.

I knew Peace Corps had three goals, and I was selfishly hoping to leave a legacy tied to at least one of them. I wanted to leave my mark, to help develop the developing world, while doing the "toughest job I would ever love." Aside from that, I deliberately held off from creating expectations. I wanted to be open to whatever came my way. I realize now I was expecting my new colleagues to know as little English as I knew Bulgarian. Luckily, they knew a lot more than me. A few of my colleagues were fluent; a couple of them didn't speak a word. They had Master's Degrees, and PhDs, and were published academics. They were all very smart people, whom I had unknowingly underestimated. While I was prepared for a language barrier, I didn't expect to be the one learning English from my Bulgarian colleagues.

As a native speaker, with a TEFL Certificate, and an English teaching practice in Ecuador, I felt confident I had something to contribute. Having grown up on a ranch in Colorado, with an International Affairs degree and travel experience, I was hopeful I might employ some of those insights as well. But, if there was nothing else I could offer in my first few months of service, I thought I could at least offer my

8

English. So, it felt good to be asked to edit the foundation's English website as one of my first tasks. Little did I know, an unspoken part of that first assignment was to not question their existing translation. As that realization set in, I had to learn some new English words. Draggle, as defined by Dictionary.com, is the verb "to make wet and dirty by dragging on the ground." A word I didn't know before is now one I will never forget. While I still wouldn't choose draggle to describe the Roma farmers we were trying to assist, they did. It was in their unedited website text, and there it would stay. Now I know that it wasn't really about draggle – it was about my expectations. I learned draggle, and my role as a volunteer. I was left scrambling to find something else I could contribute besides my English skills. What could I do to help them that they couldn't do for themselves? When I signed up to serve as a Peace Corps volunteer, I never thought I would be second guessing the assistance I could provide to my new colleagues. I never expected to be learning English from them, along with Bulgarian, and so much more.

Thinking about it now, being humbled by my colleagues, and their skills were never on my radar. I just knew I could help. My expectations were general to the Peace Corps and volunteers I had met who had served in Latin America, Africa, and Asia. I wanted an adventure. I was excited to live overseas again and excited to learn a new language. I wanted to experience a culture and geography that was completely foreign to me. I wanted to make a meaningful contribution and was willing to face hardships to make that happen. I needed to defer my student loans and to have good medical support if something came up. I wanted to be placed together with my wife for our service, if not also for Pre- Service Training.

I thought I knew a few things, but in hindsight, it was incredible how much I didn't know. A decade later, I still feel humbled at the privilege of serving as a Peace Corps volunteer.

Brian Fassett
Bulgaria
'04–'06

THE 8-STEP APPLICATION PROCESS

SO, YOU'VE MADE THE DECISION to join Peace Corps which means you're prepared to take the journey of completing the application process. I wish it were as simple as submitting just an application and waiting for an interview, but it isn't. If you're still debating about joining, remember to read some of my adventures during my service at TravelBranyik.com.

Before we get deep into the process, there is one thing I would like to mention. You can apply anytime you want, but Peace Corps recommends completing your application by January 1st. Now! Onto the fun part.

There are eight steps to the Peace Corps Application process:

- Applying Online
- Completing the Health History Form (HHF)
- Making Choices
- Completing the Soft Skills Questionnaire
- Interview
- Invitation
- Medical and Legal Clearance
- Departure

This can be a lengthy process for most, and a lot of waiting is involved. Peace Corps recommends you apply 9 – 12 months before departure. I started the entire application process in March 2013 and didn't get my invitation until January 2014. It took almost a full year for me to be invited to serve. While some who apply late in the game can get an invitation in four months, others may receive their invitation after 11 months of waiting. It depends.

The best advice I can give you is to be patient.

If the application process has you strung out, it's never too late to consult a Peace Corps recruiter. They are loaded with everything you need to help ease any anxiety you have around the application process. Luckily, you can find a recruiter most anywhere in the country, and they are always willing to help.

There are more than 70 recruiters waiting to assist you, and according to Peace Corps website, people who consult with a Peace Corps Recruiter about their opportunities are 55% more likely to be accepted into a program.

If you are struggling with the process and have questions, you can go online to find a recruiter at https://www.peacecorps.gov/volunteer/connect-with-a-recruiter/.

If you also feel like you could use some help developing your application skills, Peace Corps offers Application Workshops. Workshops are available as events through the Peace Corps website and can be found here https://www.peacecorps.gov/events/.

And now another fun part, learning about how to apply to Peace Corps in the best possible manner. Be forewarned, the application process may make you feel like your life is on hold and you things will happen that are not in your control. Don't worry that is all completely normal.

During the whole process, other juicy opportunities or events may interrupt it. You could be presented with a fantastic job opportunity, your friend could get married, you could get married, or there could be a death in the family. Many things could happen during the process that cause for delay or put your application on hold. When they do, stop and assess the moment, feel what you need to feel, and then think about your future and how to proceed.

If for some reason you do end up with a great job opportunity at your doorstep, consider which choice will be most beneficial to your future. Make a pros and cons list for the new job opportunity and the Peace Corps opportunity. If you get married, discuss with your partner the option of joining the Peace Corps together. Remember to consider all sides and all possibilities for these choices.

Sometimes the process will seem so lengthy you're inclined to give up and find something else. This is a typical feeling. I like to remind people when this happens, this is a good practice of patience. Patience is one of the many skills that will contribute to your success in service once you join Peace Corps. If you have this feeling, take some deep breaths, consider the benefits you will receive during service, and post-service, and go from there.

If you start the application process and halfway through decide, "I don't really want to do this as much as I thought," That is okay too! We are in constant motion, and patterns of growth within us can happen at times we rarely expect. When this happens, it changes how we see the world, our perspective, and even the things we desire in life. This is normal. If you liked the idea but felt Peace Corps wasn't right for you, there are plenty of other volunteer options you can be a part of. You just have to find your most suitable one.

The application process will test your patience, and at times it may seem everything is coming at you all at once. I assure you the application process is straightforward if approached with an open mind and can be smooth depending on how prepared you are.

If you complete the application process and are not accepted, contact someone and ask what you could've done differently. There are always moments where you can improve and try again.

So, how bad do you want to join the Peace Corps? If you still don't know, that's what this book is here for. To help, let's do an exercise. This can be done before or after you start your application. Take as long as you would like to write and express as much as you feel is necessary.

Begin by sitting down at a table or in a place you feel comfortable. Get out a tablet, computer, piece of paper or any medium for writing. Then, answer these three questions: Why do you want to join Peace Corps? How will it benefit you long-term? What are your goals and expectations?

I asked you to do this exercise to help you organize your thoughts and feelings around your desire to join. It will give you a visual and a piece of concrete evidence for your goals and your aspirations. At this point, you may have a lot of drive, a lot of motivation and a lot of feelings toward joining the Peace Corps. It may help to organize these emotions all in one place.

Take this exercise, tear it out of your notebook, print it out, whatever, and hang it in a place you always look. When you experience times of uncertainty, you can look back at your original goals and expectations to reassess how you feel. It's a reminder of why you started the journey in the first place.

Now that you have completed the short exercise let's take a look at how to make the application process simpler for you.

STEP 1: APPLY ONLINE
This process will take about an hour or more depending on how prepared you are. I recommend preparing for the application before you even apply.

Before you begin make sure you have these things handy:

- Basic Contact Info
- Education Info
- Social Security Number (SSN)
- Your most recent Resume/CV
- Motivation Statement
- Two References (Close Friend and Job-Related)

The application asks for your basic contact info first, which is easy as pie. I recommend focusing on the Motivation Statement. The Motivation Statement is a short essay your recruiter will use to assess if you are an appropriate candidate for Peace Corps.

Instead of just shooting from the hip on this one, take a few hours or even a day to write out your Motivation Statement. Again, sit down in a comfortable place with your preferred writing medium and express in totality your intentions for joining Peace Corps.

What's really cool about this, is you completed this earlier in the chapter! Use that exercise if you need a little help. Otherwise, the Motivation Statement as written straight from the online application is below:

Peace Corps service presents major physical, emotional, and intellectual challenges. In the space below, please provide a few paragraphs explaining your reasons for wanting to serve as a Peace Corps Volunteer and how you plan to overcome the various challenges associated with Peace Corps service. This essay is the writing sample Peace Corps uses to assess your professionalism and maturity as a candidate. Please spend time editing your essay/writing sample (up to 500 words).

STEPS 2 - 4: THE HEALTH AND HISTORY FORM, MAKE SOME CHOICES, SOFT SKILLS QUESTIONNAIRE

Whew! You have completed the easy part. The next two parts are also going to be very easy in comparison to everything else.

This is the part where Peace Corps will ask you to fill out a Health History Form (HHF) and ask you to choose the country of service you desire.

It is best to be honest about everything in your health history. Peace Corps will determine the best country of service for you based on your health, and where you are passionate about going.

It's imperative to fill out the HHF in absolute truth. If something medically related happened to you in your country of service and Peace Corps was unaware of this condition, it could pose a problem getting you the help you need in remote places. Peace Corps needs to make sure you are physically and mentally capable of completing your goals as a volunteer. Don't be shy and tell the truth. Peace Corps will take care of you. They excel at caring for their volunteers.

Health History Form (HHF)

For step two of the process, they recommend you complete this part very quickly so they can start the more critical parts of your application process – finding a place for you in Peace Corps.

When I completed this part, it was a challenge because I have been unvaccinated for most of my adult life. When it came time to do my Final Medical Clearance, I was running around like crazy, paying tons of cash to get these shots and immunizations. I had to dig up my past and had no records of vaccinations I got as a child. I had to get shots again.

If by chance you are anything like me, you are probably going to need your necessary shots for measles, the flu, chicken pox, and other grand stuff. Peace Corps will not allow you to serve if you don't have the necessary shots and immunizations.

Every country of service is different, some shots and immunizations are required, and others are not. It just depends. Be prepared no matter your circumstances.

You won't really know about the details of your final medical clearance until you accept your invitation. I know this may not be what you want to hear, but be patient, and all will be good.

If you prefer, I suggest you stay up to date with your regular shots and go to the dentist regularly to save yourself some time with the entire medical process. Be proactive and be ready when the time comes.

Make Some Choices
Step three of the process requires you to choose your country of service. My group, the China 20s, didn't have the option to choose our country of service in 2013. I was randomly placed in China. My recruiter asked me where I wanted to go if I had the choice. I had no plan or idea. I figured where Peace Corps placed me was where I needed to be. Lucky for you, you get to choose where you want to go. There is some advantage in that. You may be able to keep your final destination a mystery if you're up for that!

It's helpful getting to choose on your own because you can select a country that you already have a skill in. I had very few skills, other than my English education, and I happened to have a degree in English. But when I went to China, I had no teaching skills and no Chinese skills. Not having been prepped with those skills posed major challenges for me.

16

If you do have a particular skill with health, education, the environment, or even with languages like Chinese, Spanish, French, etc., you already have a significant advantage in choosing a country of service.

Of course, this is all just my opinion, if you feel like totally waltzing blind into your service like I did, I applaud you for your bravery. It may not be easy, but you will be an awesome, well-rounded person afterward. If you do know the country of service, you would like to apply for, wonderful! If you really desire to be a volunteer but find you don't know which area you would like to volunteer for, start writing out your thoughts.

> Sit in a comfortable place with your desired medium for writing. Go to PeaceCorps.gov and find the list of programs available for service. Take a few minutes to review the programs. Now, answer this question: What top three programs are most interesting to you? List one reason for each program you wrote down. Next, answer this question: Which program will be most beneficial to my future and my personal goals?

If making a decision right away or even writing it down makes you nervous, take a day or two or three to think about what you would like to do and what your passion is.

If you are a pro at English, China might be a suitable place for you. If you are the type of person who really cares about personal health and has an incredible amount of knowledge on this topic, Peru would be a great choice. Maybe you have great care and concern for our environment and want to pass on your knowledge to the world, then a place like Togo may be your best bet.

If after a few days, you feel like you still don't know what program you would like to be a part of, there are Peace Corps groups on Facebook full of volunteers with great experiences ready to share their stories with you. And never underestimate The Google. After my service, the Google became a great resource for finding volunteers who run their own blogs.

After reading through various blogs about volunteers in different countries of service, you may discover which experience will suit you best. Remember, not all experiences are alike. It depends, and that, my friends, is the beauty of life.

Soft Skills Questionnaire

Some of you might be wondering about step four and what it is. What are soft skills? I didn't know what soft skills were or that employers even looked at those things until my service was almost over and we were discussing resumes and cover letters. During service, you'll gain more skills than you'll know what to do with, but you'll still need to demonstrate your current and strongest ones when interviewing.

When making resumes and cover letters, you will be including a wide variety of all the skills you have gained through schooling or through experiencing life.

Hard skills are the teachable abilities you gain like language, math, science, typing, or how to use software programs. Soft skills are abilities less concrete, something you can't really quantify like, flexibility, working well with others, patience, etc. Peace Corps will again ask you to fill out this questionnaire as soon as possible so they can continue reviewing you as an appropriate candidate for service.

If you are struggling with this portion of the questionnaire because you are uncertain of what skills you have, think about anything you ever participated in – school clubs, community volunteer programs, jobs, or other miscellaneous projects.

Make a list of all the tasks you've completed or all the things you had to do during these projects. I'll give you an example.

I worked as a server during college. I know what you are thinking, how does working as a server give you skills that could ready you for Peace Corps? Here's a list of skills I gained working as a server.

These are a few examples of both Hard Skills and Soft Skills I gained as a server. There are very few but look at the soft skills. They are all very beneficial to work as a volunteer.

Hard Skills	Soft Skills
Aloha Software	Working With Others
Cash Handling	Communication
Spanish Speaker	Multitasking

In Peace Corps, you will be 'working with others' to complete your primary goals and to organize projects. You will need to learn how to 'communicate' effectively with your counterparts as well as Peace Corps staff to complete most of these goals, especially if you face challenges. There may be times you need to be a good 'multitasker' during service.

Some volunteers in China were constantly involved in English related projects and clubs in addition to their primary goal of teaching English. This requires much attention outside of the classroom and more lesson planning.

Most China Volunteers are heavily invested in English clubs, reading clubs, fitness clubs, drama clubs, and English corners. These projects together need attention and require you to multitask.

Why is it important to assess the soft skills appropriately? Because they contribute greatly to your overall success as a volunteer. If I'd had a better grasp on patience, there is little doubt my job as a volunteer at the beginning of my service would have been much smoother. Lesson learned.

Peace Corps needs to know these skills so they can determine if you are an appropriate fit for the program you desire. They need to know if you work well with others, if you are flexible, and if you are good at communicating.

Peace Corps will want to present a volunteer to a school who is very excited to be there. HCNs collaborating with a difficult volunteer may decide in the future that they don't want to host another volunteer let alone be part of Peace Corps Programs.

Our host countries look for willing, open-minded, dedicated, and motivated volunteers. Keep this in mind. Let's exercise again.

Choose a job or project you have done either in school or for a company and make two columns, one for Hard Skills and one for Soft Skills. Add the appropriate skills to the appropriate columns. Take your time and really give thought to the kind of employee or worker you were. What kind of attitude did you have? Were you helpful? What were your strongest abilities? Recall any compliments and accolades your employer, supervisor, teacher, or coworker gave you during this project or job.

STEP 5: INTERVIEW
After completing the first four steps, a month or so may have passed. Doesn't seem like much time at all since you've probably been so busy thinking about the entire process of joining and the anticipation of getting accepted. The anticipation will get much stronger once you are called for your interview. Don't panic! This can be an exciting part! I know it was for me.

You'll get an email saying you have been selected to be interviewed and they will send you to the nearest location from where you are, or they will set up a video conference. Be prepared for to travel a little, I was from a small town in southern Colorado and drove to Denver for my interview.

The interview can be stressful, and you want to say the right things, so the recruiter nominates you for a program. This part is awesome because you get to tell the Peace Corps recruiter all about your passions, your goals, your failures, your expectations, and your desires for growth. During the interview, they will really get into your biggest failures and your favorite accomplishments to get a better understanding of you, which is unlike your normal interview. The recruiters are looking for what makes you genuine and how your past experiences have influenced your present and future. This is your chance to shine your light and show how amazing you are.

Keep your thoughts in order, write down a few things you would like to say and consider some of the questions Peace Corps might ask you. How will you answer them? Here is the list of questions to consider when preparing for your interview.

- Why are you right for Peace Corps?
- What are your goals for joining Peace Corps?
- Why did you choose your specific program?
- What you will gain from Peace Corps?
- How will you face challenges in Peace Corps?
- What soft skills do you have that will benefit your service?

Practice reciting these topics with someone you trust, like your parents, guardians, professors, friends, siblings, or whoever supports you. If you aren't comfortable with this, you can practice in front of a mirror. If your loved ones have critiques for you, allow them to give you the critiques and be open to them. Let them help you prepare for your interview so you can totally rock it when the time comes.

When you have finally reached the day you will interview, remember to dress professionally. The way you present yourself can make or break your nomination. Go to your interview dressed for success in business casual attire, combed hair, and a smile. If you have body art, try to cover it as much as you can. Some countries of service may view tattoos as a taboo. However, recruiters most likely will not take tattoos into consideration when interviewing you. Professionalism is key.

Do all this, and you'll improve your chances of getting nominated. If you're lucky, the recruiter may tell you right then if they've decided to nominate you or not!

STEP 6 AND 7: INVITATION AND MEDICAL CLEARANCE
When I did my interview, it went so well I was sure Peace Corps would call me immediately and invite me to serve. I was confident about my interview.

I went to my Peace Corps application portal daily to check the status of my application, obsessed with finding out if I was chosen for a country of service. I started the process in March 2013, had the Interview in May, and got nominated a few weeks after my interview. Then it was silence for the next seven months. I was so anxious. I started looking for other jobs and opportunities.

I applied for the world traveler contest where you make a video about traveling around the world for $100,000 a year. I created a short stop-action video that I drew on paper with a Sharpie. I took photos of each shot, pieced them together and sent it in. It took up a lot of the time and energy I had been putting into worrying about Peace Corps. I didn't win, and then it was back to square one.

The length of time between Interview and Invitation may test your patience and confidence. You may consider other options or more realistic ones because you think Peace Corps is just taking too long. This is a completely normal feeling, and if you do have it, I suggest you look back at that exercise we did on page 17 assessing why you wanted to join Peace Corps in the first place. Sometimes it helps to revisit your goal.

It's easy to get obsessed and worried during this large gap between notifications. Do your best to just go with it. If you are working, stay focused on your job, read books, continue with life. For me, I spent over a year working four jobs, paying down loans and credit card debt, so I had less to worry about when I was serving.

I saved a good chunk of money for the sake of paying loans, I spent time with my family and friends, and I did all the fun recreational activities I really loved doing just in the case I missed them when I left. I was still confident I would be invited despite my anxiety about the application process. Stay focused and confident. Live your life while you wait.

During the application process, it was helpful to keep a journal. You'll notice I've suggested you keep one. People may not understand the stress and worry you feel around waiting, you may not understand it yourself, but your journal does. My friends didn't believe I was crazy enough to do Peace Corps until I got my Invitation. They didn't think I would go through with it. Get a journal. Your journal will never dismiss your feelings of anxiety around joining Peace Corps. Your journal understands you.

When that Invitation finally arrived, I was at job number two for the day, tagging clothes at a clothing store. There was never cell service in the warehouse where I was tagging clothes, yet the email came through. I remember the moment I looked at my phone and saw the email from Peace Corps. I stopped all things I was doing to read it. I learned I was being invited to China. I stood in the back of the warehouse trying to carry on with my job, smiling like an idiot and then suddenly I began to cry. This meant I was going around the world and away from my family. This feeling lasted about a minute before I transitioned to worry. The "I-don't-know-about-China" kind of worry. It was glorious!

Before you accept your Invitation, they ask you to read through documents about the country of service you have been invited to live in.

It's exciting to finally read through all the paperwork, tell your family, tell your friends, and even your coworkers. They might be overwhelmed with emotion just like you are. They might be terrified too. If you need to, talk to them about where you are about to serve, educate them on what is next, and try to get them as excited as you know you are.
Heck, even gift them this book to help them understand the process. Accept or decline your Invitation and be prepared for what is next.

After you accept your Invitation, Peace Corps will bombard your inbox with emails almost every single day about what you need to do next. I have a few tips for keeping this chaos at bay.

Organize Your Inbox

I suggest creating a whole folder in your inbox just for Peace Corps emails. You will get so many! You don't want to lose or overlook any of them. The last thing you want is to forget to complete a task because of a lost email.

Create a To-Do List

As the emails come at you full force with tasks you need complete, start making a list of each with the date it is due in order of urgency. This will keep you from getting anything confused, so you don't miss a task.

This is another reason a journal comes handy. If you want to get really crazy, you organize your tasks into categories using an Excel spreadsheet!

Build A Binder of Documents

I left my parents in charge of any legal documents, medical documents, passport copies, bank account info, SSN, Birth Certificate, diplomas, etc. so that if I was ever in a jam Peace Corps couldn't assist with, I could contact my parents and ask them to send things over.

I placed everything in a binder and gave it to them. Over time, they added things to it, copies of my x-rays, addresses, letters, etc. I even put a journal in the back for them just in case they felt like writing about their experience as parents with a daughter in Peace Corps.

Schedule School Loan Deferments

If you just finished college, have student loans and need to make deferments, get this process going. Once you reach the eighth step of Orientation, Peace Corps staff will give you an official document to send to your loan company for proof of deferment. Best to start the deferment process early on to relieve any issues there.

Collect Resumes, Cover Letters, and Diplomas

Take some time to piece together a folder with your current resume, cover letter, and diplomas. Your host school may ask you for these once you arrive. It is best to make 2 – 3 folders with one copy of each document if one or more parties need them.

Try to keep them as up to date as possible. Place them in plastic folders because you never know what things could explode in your suitcase on the flight over.

Complete Final Medical and Dental Clearance
Once you have accepted your Invitation, you will be asked to complete the Final Medical Clearance.

This part involves things like blood tests, immunizations, dental exams, physical exams, all of it. It may take a while. It is important to stay focused and organized for this part.

If you don't do this part right, you will be asked to do it again. If you make an error on the paperwork or document, miss a piece of information or send incomplete documents, you will have to redo the paperwork, x-ray, whatever, and then send it back to the staff handling everything.

Make it easy on the PC staff and yourself. Chances are, your group is large, so they are dealing with a lot of people at once.

Try to group several medical tasks together for one day over a few weeks. If you try to do them all in one day, it probably won't happen. If you have access to it, try using a local health clinic. If you have a lower income, you may be able to receive your exams or shots at reduced prices.

Free health clinics sometimes provide services if your income is below a certain point. That being said, Peace Corps pays for most all medical and dental work you will have to do to be cleared for service. I still had to pay more than $200 out of pocket for some services, so be prepared for this.

For your help, and this may change, I put together a list of things to pay attention to as you fill out paperwork for medical and dental clearance.

- Medical Clearance Requirements from Office (Check each task off list when fully complete)
- Fill out forms, check all boxes, and Doc Sign all forms in their entirety
- 2 Physical Forms Completed (Please place Doctor's Signature and Office stamp on both Physical Forms)
- Sign Health History Form (HHF) Forms
- Chest X-Ray w/ Radiology Report and Digital Copies of X-Ray

- EKG and Interpretation
- Tests to complete:
    o HIV
    o Syphilis
    o Hep B Antigen
    o RPR
    o G6PD Titer
    o Metabolic Panel
    o Hep C
    o TB
    o CBC
    o Urinalysis
- Billing department should complete an itemized bill on a UB-92, HCF A-1500, or ADA form which will be sent to Peace Corps Office to Reimburse doctor's office (provided by doctors).

If you stay organized, you will experience more ease completing the final steps of getting out of Dodge. You will avoid doing tedious tasks over again.

If you have snags in your paperwork or the whole process and feel emotional and stressed out, get your journal out, and write away! Never hesitate to call the Peace Corps Staff member tending to your group, they will help you and answer questions regarding this process. Plus, they are helpful and wonderful!

STEP 8: DEPARTURE AND ORIENTATION

You've done it! You have made it all the way to Orientation, assuming you booked your flight with Peace Corps, and you will soon be taking the big exciting leap moving across the world to join other dedicated volunteers already serving. Congratulations! Are you ready?

What happens at this point? Once you arrive at Orientation, you will take part in a day of training preparing you for your departure as well as group activities to ease your nerves before getting on the plane.

But that's probably not what you are most nervous about at this point.

Everyone's worry at this point is how to pack appropriately. Generally, you're allowed a personal bag, carry-on and two checked bags no more than 50 pounds, so keep this in mind when packing.

This is a great time to rely on your veteran volunteers and Facebook groups. You will be able to connect with other groups serving in your country of service and ask for advice on what to bring with you. Every country will have different suggestions. China, for example, is a lot urbaner and developed than other countries. We were afforded many luxuries other countries were not. We even had Wal-Marts in some places. But if I needed clothing, I bought it or had it made in China. It was easier to acquire items in China whereas other places with volunteers serving in more rural areas like Nicaragua may have fewer options.

Talk to volunteers currently living in your country of service. They can give you so much more advice and save you the stress of carrying too much while you travel.

Packing, Unpacking, and Repacking

I chose to pack three months before departure. I packed and unpacked several times before leaving. I wanted to make sure I had everything I needed. While repacking, I discovered I had added something I didn't really need, although I thought I needed it before. After a year in Peace Corps, there were things I brought with me I hadn't used since I arrived in China.

Sometimes other things are added to your suitcase last minute. My father insisted I pack a sleeping bag "just in case." It took up half my suitcase, which I had made space for after packing and repacking several times. I only used it once, but I'm glad he made me pack it. Be mindful and realistic about what you need by packing, unpacking, and repacking a few times.

Better To Pack Light

In China, we moved our bags three times in 12 weeks. It was torture. China had no elevators, so it was brutal moving multiple bags full of our lives from place to place. I moved three bags up six flights of stairs to my host sister's apartment.

At one point, she stopped helping me. After you make it through training, PC Staff will probably give you extra equipment to take to your permanent site. So, seriously pack light, so you don't die from exertion. Invest in hard-shell suitcases because they tend to weigh half as much as the soft-shell cases. You can also pack things more effectively.

Relax. It's Orientation

This part is a weird sort of mingling time between you and the other volunteers and managing your emotions around leaving. It will be awesome, and you will have a great time meeting your fellow volunteers. You will do little bits of paperwork for loan deferments and such, and then, Peace Corps will give you some money for travel. Within the next day or two, you will hop on a plane with your fellow trainees and go off on your adventure.

The Application process is one of the toughest parts of joining the Peace

Corps, and you did it! You will soon forget it and focus on more exciting things like PST, another exciting adventure full of Technical Training, Language Training, and Cross-Cultural Training.

I hope that while you are completing the Application Process, you are documenting it somehow. Many people considering Peace Corps are out there looking for information, and you could be sharing it. Not everyone will resonate with my experience, but they might resonate with yours. Keep a journal, a blog, a vlog, or whatever is easiest. You may be of help to all the other people out there considering Peace Corps. Again, Congratulations on completing the Application process!

PRE-SERVICE TRAINING (PST)

THE PEACE CORPS CHINA 20S GROUP met in Los Angeles June 2014 for orientation at a hotel not far from In-And-Out Burger. I remember sitting at a long table in the lobby of the hotel, watching all the volunteers walk upstairs, through the lounge, and maneuver through a maze of large suitcases. That afternoon, I could barely swallow the first In-And-Out burger I had ever experienced in my life. People must've thought I was crazy.

Orientation, the last step of the Application Process, lasted only a day before we were off to the airport again to prepare for more than a day's worth of travel. We went from L.A. to Bangkok, to Tokyo, to Chengdu and all without someone to lead our group. All 83 Peace Corps China Trainees lined up against the wall in the airport just before the check-in, eager to get through security and to our gate. A lady at the check-in single-handedly took over four hours to check-in all 83 volunteers. While we all waited patiently to check in, those who made it through security, had the luxury of enjoying the FIFA world cup and relaxing in the terminal. The check-in time was so long the plane had to wait for the rest of us. Two gentlemen in our group made sure everyone got through.

Upon arriving in Bangkok, and without a Peace Corps rep leading our group, we experienced a 6-hour layover. We randomly got on a bus we believed was for us and went to a hotel for the night. How we knew where we were going was beyond me.

We passed by buildings covered by the dark night until we arrived at the hotel. It was a cozy and luxurious four hours of sleep before we got up at the crack of dawn to head back to the airport.

Later that morning, we arrived in Chengdu, and it was a lot gloomier than I expected and dirty. The signs were all Chinese like little drawings and cars pushed passed the bus on either side. I was terrified. This was the farthest I had ever been away from home, and it finally hit me that I wasn't in Colorado anymore.

We showed up with expectations of our hotel, fear of the squat toilets, which one of the volunteers would be our next husband or wife, and excited to learn what Peace Corps was all about. Putting aside the juicy sexual tension that happens when you place 83 volunteers together in the same hotel living space for two weeks, PST is jam-packed with all kinds of prep you should be paying attention to for the sake of improving your service.

I remember feeling totally lost during the first two weeks of our intense training. The medical and security staff were pounding information into our brains. I was occupied with a combination of jet lag and the super fun immunizations they pump into both arms upon your arrival into the country. More than anything, this was the farthest I had ever been from home and the farthest I was from my comfort zone. I was nervous, scared, and out of it.

PST is a lot to take in and a blur. You are given at least three very large and important tasks that become the center of PST, to begin with, Language Training, Cross-Cultural Training, and In-Service Skills Training (teaching, health, agriculture, etc.). You are excited, nervous, and for 10 to 12 weeks you are in sessions all day long getting comfortable with saying "Hello" one million times in the language and hearing medical staff talk about unavoidable diarrhea you will experience as you shift to new and exotic foods. Remember to take notes, take lots of notes.

For the first two weeks of your PST experience, you will most likely be in a hotel or area where all volunteers can come together to participate in training. You will finish getting your in-country immunizations and vaccinations, and then two weeks later, the Peace Corps staff may place you at a training site and with a host family that will care for you for the next 10 to 12 weeks of your training.

For China, we stayed with our host families for 10 to 12 weeks and then went to our two-year permanent site. Some volunteers, depending on the country, may be living with their host family for the duration of their service.

If you like your own space, or you like being around lots of people, best to consider these things when applying for Peace Corps. Be open to the possibilities of meeting new people and experiencing new things. Closing yourself off to opportunities could keep you from growing and experiencing everything in your host country.

PST OVERVIEW

The Peace Corps Staff will conduct the Pre-Service Training for a two month period. They make sure you arrive safely in-country and that you are well taken care of up until the time of your Close of Service and Departure. The Peace Corps Staff will be a combination of locally hired trainers, current volunteers, and trained staff from the United States.

During the time you are in training, the staff will measure your language competencies, learning achievements, and a relatively solid grasp of cross-cultural understanding, and health and safety precautions.

They also make sure you are integrating into the community properly, which I why Peace Corps instills a homestay experience within Pre-Service Training to help you develop your language outside of the classroom and begin your individual understanding of the cultural.

A combination of these assessments will help the staff determine if you need extra assistance developing skills like language and teaching which are important things that will help you have a successful service.

2-WEEK MODEL SCHOOL

If you're an English teacher serving in China, all volunteers at your training site will get involved in what we call, Model School. You partner with another volunteer in your training school and practice the teaching skills you have learned during PST.

You have the opportunity to work with kids who volunteered to be your students for Model School.

The benefits of Model School is, you get to test out and lesson plans you have drawn up, you get a little taste of what an HCN's learning style is like, and you get to practice your presence as a teacher.

Your teacher-trainers will be with along the way, give you helpful tools o assist you through Model School, and answer any questions you may have on how to improve your teaching skills. More importantly, the teacher trainers are most likely RPCVs who have a greater knowledge of the learning styles of your students.

The one downside of Model School is that the level of English you are working with, may not reflect the students you will actually be teaching at your permanent site. It depends on whether you go to a major University or a small high school.

For example, the students at my permanent site had much lower English than the students I had in Model School. There was no way I could've prepared for that or known that. My advice to you there is to just be ready for any possibility and don't set too high of expectations!

TECHNICAL TRAINING

So, maybe you are one of the volunteers who joined Peace Corps to develop some of the best skills you already have. And because Peace Corps loves you, they're going to make sure you develop your skills so you can further your career.

Whether it is dealing with agricultural skills, grant writing skills, teaching skills, international relations, Peace Corps will help you develop them in the most effective way, so you get even more out of your service.

HEALTH TRAINING
Peace Corps staff takes your health very seriously. I won't lie to you, there have been cases of Peace Corps volunteers with compromised health while they are in service, and some have passed away, but it is extremely rare. That's why Peace Corps Staff will do whatever it takes to provide you with preventative measures to make sure you are in good health for the duration of your service.

You will be involved in lengthy trainings that detail nutrition, consumption of water, food preparation, alcohol and drug awareness, emotional health, domestic violence, and whatever else you need to stay healthy during your service. They also tackle topics around sexual intercourse, HIV/AIDS, and other sexually transmitted diseases. Training you on how to respond to emergencies when you are ill is also a very big part of the training.

SAFETY AND SECURITY TRAINING
All countries in the world have places they consider dangerous, and that's just the reality of the world. That being said, Peace Corps would not deliberately send you to a place where your safety could be compromised.

Regardless, Peace Corps is obligated to make sure you are safe abroad, which will also give your family and friends back home a piece of mind. The PC staff is 100% responsible for anything that happens to you, so they train you on how to reduce safety risks you may experience at home, at school, or while you are traveling. They will teach you how to extinguish safety risks you may experience in-country that refer to gender issues, transportation safety, emergency action planning, dealing with unwanted attention, and bystander intervention.

CROSS-CULTURAL TRAINING
Understanding the culture you are about to live in for the next two years, is something they focus heavily on in training. This will be your crash course to understanding, but you will learn much more about your host country as your service goes on.

During these trainings, Peace Corps staff will address any questions you have about the behaviors, practices, and the underlying reasons for those behaviors and practices in the culture. Peace Corps staff will address topics like communication styles, hierarchies, gender roles, and relationship dynamics.

Host Family experiences are a wonderful part of service, and it is a great place to know more about HCNs and your host country. It is a safe environment that allows you to learn the customs and habits of the culture while being patient and compassionate about your integration.

During my first encounter with my host parents, who did not speak English, my host dad told me he didn't like the Chinese name given to me by my language coaches. That same day, he came up with a new Chinese name for me, one that suited me better. He even blessed me with his surname, which was a great honor.

By the time my 10 weeks of living with my host family was completed, we were all in tears as I departed to my permanent site in Chongqing. That was how strong our bond had developed. I had grown to love them as my family and vice versa.

Friends and family can be a big part of service and big support while our other families are thousands of miles away. Jacqueline shared a story about how closely bonded she was with her family in her country of service and what it felt like leaving them at the end.

There is no greater experience than being accepted with open arms into another person's family – being fully engulfed in their day-to-day activities, celebrations, and mournings. The day I walked into Keur Serigne Thioye, exhausted from the long journey and with the vocabulary of a toddler, I was immediately embraced as my mother's daughter, my brother's sister, and my aunt's niece. In fact, my entire family of twenty-two rushed into the hut to meet, welcome, and stare at this new family member. When my nephew crawled into my lap, offered me a piece of his mango, and then refused to move, I knew that I was truly at home.

This family grew to be an essential part of my life in Senegal. During the first few weeks, it was my mother who escorted me to all the neighbors and told them about my service as a Peace Corps Volunteer. It was my father who quickly learned to understand my quirky Americanized Wolof and helped me to improve my language abilities. It was my aunt who took me to visit her friends and introduced me to teenage Senegalese life. And it was the children who constantly entertained me and were always ready to learn American games or to teach me Senegalese ones.

As time continued, it was also my family that I turned to for stability and comfort. Every evening, riding home on my bike or walking back from the closest town, my 3-year-old nephew would run down the road, shouting, "Aida, nyo na! Aida, nyo na!" (Aida has come home!) He would race on his short legs down the path and wait to be whisked into my arms. He would then follow me into my room, rolling on my bed, and dutifully sharing the lunch leftovers handed to me by my sister.

During the evening, while women prepared dinner, I would lie outside, star gazing with my brothers and telling fairy tales to the children.

Living in a foreign country, in a culture vastly different from my own, creating my own schedule and work responsibilities, it was the stability of my family life that I looked forward to every evening. No matter the struggles of the day, I loved coming back home.

My family looked out for me in a way that would make my American mother proud. One day, a fellow PCV came to visit me, and we decided to visit a nearby fishing village (about 9 km away) with a legendary mountain so tall, if you could climb it, you'd be able to see all the way to Banjul. My mother gave us directions, and we set off down the path. We had been walking for about an hour when my friend turned around and did a double take. "Is that your mother?" She asked and pointed to a woman running in the distance. I turned, and sure enough, it was mother; she had raced after us, afraid that we'd miss the side path in the dirt road that would take us to our destination. She then continued to accompany us for a few kilometers until she was confident that we would not get lost. My friend and I eventually made it to the village, found the mountain which was more like a hill, climbed to the top, and saw all the way to… The trees across the river.

When it came time for Close of Service and departing from Senegal, leaving my family was the hardest thing I have ever done in my life. Now 4000 miles away, I still consider them my family and think of them every day.

Jacqueline Gerson
Senegal '12 – '14

Beautiful stories like this remind us that all experiences with volunteers are different. Some go into the host country with little or no knowledge about the country, the language, or the skills needed for effective service. Then there are some who have training in these skills, training in the language, or heavy knowledge of their country of service. Regardless, we are accepted and taken care of like family. How this plays out depends on the person and the place.

SWEARING INTO PEACE CORPS SERVICE

As you wrap your training, the PC staff will move you from your homestay to a hotel so you can complete your training and swear in.

They will organize a large ceremony with guest speakers from the Embassy, Peace Corps, and your group of volunteers. You will take the oath to carry out your service to the best of your ability in-country and then you will enjoy a meal with your fellow volunteers and enjoy the speeches from your guest speakers.

This will be the last time you see your host family for a while, but it will also be the first time you meet your counterparts and supervisors from the school hosting you at your permanent site.

You'll meet and greet, and they will help you transport any Peace Corps equipment you've been issued to take with you to your site. That is when another great phase of your adventure begins.

Be open-minded about what is to come, and you will have an amazing experience in PST and with your host family much like in Jacqueline's story. Your efforts in PST and your outlooks on your service to come will start with optimism and ways of looking at the world. Your attitude, whether positive or negative, will be the reason your service is bad, good, or great! If you need help getting to that open-minded point, remember to reference the stories I have shared during my Peace Corps service at TravelBranyik.com. You can also confide in your host family, the PC staff or other PCVs to help you through this exciting journey.

LEARNING LANGUAGE LIKE A PRO

LANGUAGE was one of the most important things to me and the one thing I developed most while I lived in China. There were several people in my China group with incredible Chinese Mandarin skills who were non-comparable to anything I had ever heard. I had no experience with Chinese at all, which, in the beginning, made service difficult for me. I had heard it was the hardest language in the world and the word 'hardest' was truly an understatement.

With Peace Corps, there may be a language requirement for you depending on where you serve. Some countries of service may require you to speak fluently in the mother tongue while others are a little more laid back. It depends.

If you are hoping to serve in a country that has specific requirements to be more fluent, you will be asked to demonstrate your language abilities during your interview.

If you don't have proficiency in any language, Peace Corps offers options to serve in sectors that allow you to the learn the language in-country.

Peace Corps China was broken into three levels of language learning, Novice, Intermediate, and Advanced. Each of those levels had three sublevels; Low, Middle, and High. By the end of PST, all trainees were required to reach Novice High to be considered capable of surviving in-country on their own. If they don't reach this requirement, it simply means they need more tutoring to improve this skill. Bottom line, practice, practice, practice.

Chinese is a tonal language, written in character form, and requires pinyin (a form of pronunciation given to each character). In addition to that, Chinese Mandarin is not the language spoken in most regions, although it is the national language. Each region has a specific dialect deriving from the basic Mandarin language. They have Beijing dialect, Shanghai dialect, Shenzhen dialect, Chongqing dialect, and so on and so on and so on.

HCNs speak these regional dialects more than they speak Chinese Mandarin. This meant that in our training, we were learning to speak and listen to Chinese Mandarin, but out in the world, we would have to develop our own understanding of the local language. It was an incredible challenge. By the end of PST, I had barely achieved the level of Novice High. I was so thankful, but in some ways, I needed more.

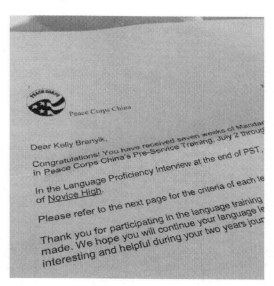

After going from Trainee to Volunteer, we were sent to our permanent sites in our specific regions. That was when I was placed in a unique situation.

Little did I know my service could and would only be improved once my language skills developed.

I had no language or teaching skills upon coming to China. I was placed at a site as their first ever volunteer. It was a vocational tourism high school full of students with severely low levels of English. The district I was living and working in had no other foreigners. I had no site mate or partner at the school with me. I was literally on my own. It was the perfect combination of everything that could make my service a nightmare. I didn't even know this kind of situation could happen to a volunteer, especially when there were much more qualified volunteers just hanging around in my group. Spoiler alert, it was hard, but it turned out to be magnificent, and this scenario is unique to most other volunteers around the globe.

Every volunteer had a site that was uniquely perfect, but there always managed to be one aspect that was challenging. Some volunteers had amazing students they connected with and successful secondary projects, but they struggled with their community outside of school. Some people had wonderful apartments but lived an hour walk or bike ride from their school.

Some people had a willing staff ready to support them in their teaching, or some had non-existent staff. For me, I had the nicest apartment I've ever inhabited in my entire life. I lived across the street from a Starbucks, Walmart, H&M, a gym, and I was a two- minute walk from my front door to the front door of the school. It was the language and cultural barriers which posed a great challenge for my teaching skills.

Never had I walked into a room, opened my mouth and been misunderstood when I spoke. I went home in tears after the first day of school. I wondered how a low-level Chinese speaker like me could teach low-level English learners like them.

It was a weird sort of plan that was set before me and there were many moments when I felt like quitting. Instead, I gained something else. Motivation.

I wanted so badly to be understood by my students and so badly wanted to make friends, that I studied reading and writing for hours a day at coffee shops. After studying, I would go out to talk to the locals at the store, the locals in my gym, go out to eat and converse with restaurant owners, or go out traveling and practice speaking with strangers.

After 6 months of spitting out incomplete sentences, incorrect tones and failing hard at listening, I reached a high point: the ability to distinguish between words. This doesn't sound monumental by any means, but it was when I knew I was making progress. From there, it was easy to plug in or pick out words or listen to a person talk and ask questions in response. Things got easier. Talking to my students was easier, making friends was easier, and I gained something else in addition to language development: cultural knowledge.

I wish Peace Corps would've stressed this more to me and all other volunteers. With language comes an understanding of culture. With learning the language, you can understand the cultures, the habits, people's gestures and postures, and the customs of the culture. And I don't just mean you learn culture by hearing stories. You learn how people interact with each other using language, how their language evolves over time with each generation, and how it has been affected and influenced over time. You learn this, and you start to connect with people, understand who they are and where they come from.

This is why language should be a central focus while at your site. Some may argue you don't need it as much, and some completely get by without it, but it is what improved all areas of my service. By the time I finished my two years of service, I had reached the Intermediate-High level of Chinese Oral Language.

The more you learn the language, the more you learn the culture. The more you understand your host country, the more open-minded you become to your environment, surroundings, and people in your community.

So, how do you learn language effectively? Many would say learning the language before you leave the U.S. is beneficial. Some say that you should wait until you are in the country to learn the language, so the environment is authentic. In my opinion, it depends on your own learning style, but for me, I know that learning the language in-country was far more beneficial for me simply because I had the environment to practice my skills.

By learning in-country, I felt like I picked up authentic habits of speaking. If I'd learned the language in America, I might have picked up less fluent habits. Bottom line, you never know how much of the language you will learn until you have no choice but to use it, and there were situations for me where it was either you speak Chinese, or you don't communicate at all.

Here are a few suggestions for learning your host-country language.

LEARNING STYLE
First, decide what type of learning style you have first. Some people can hear a word, and it immediately sticks. Some people need to see the word for it to stick. Some people need to write the word for it to stick. Then there are those types of people who need to see it, hear it, and write it before it can be remembered.

Perhaps you are the type of person who learns best with a tutor. Perhaps you just suck up all knowledge like a sponge. Think about what is easiest for you when it comes to learning, and that will be your guide. Luckily, Peace Corps is great at providing language coaches who speak to all areas of learning, visual, audio, kinesthetic, etc.

LEARNING MATERIALS
When you are accepted into Peace Corps, you will be invited to a Facebook group of in-service volunteers who are ready to welcome you into the country. Those volunteers are already 1 – 2 years into their service. They probably know some tricks. Do some networking and ask around. Rely on your fellow PCVs to give you some ideas of what methods for learning you can consider before arriving in-country as well as living in-country. They will know how to look for alternatives.

There are many resources out there, free and easy to use. Rosetta Stone is a great one but can be very costly. I like an online language resource called Mango. It is equipped with all languages imaginable. It appeals to all styles of learning so you can get the most out of your program and it comes in app form. I discovered I can access this online language learning program for free and through my public library's website. Ask your library if they provide free online language learning programs like Mango and get started if you are anxious to learn!

ANKI APP
If you are taking a smartphone with you to wherever you are serving, and find you are incredibly passionate about honing your language skills, you can also download the Anki App. It is a flashcard app that allows you to store and review all the vocabulary and grammar you are learning as you develop your language skills. With each flash card, you can decide which words are easy to remember and which ones require more review and study. It's convenient because you don't have to carry index cards everywhere you go. It is incredibly convenient for long travel by plane, train, or bus.

TEXTING AND MESSAGING APPS
The amount of time I spent texting and messaging people in Chinese was a large contributor to my overall success with learning to read, write, and listen. The messaging app I used is called WeChat, and while it is designed by the Chinese, it has a function that allows you to translate text messages from one language to the other. Check with some other volunteers currently in-service where you will be living and see if there are messaging apps you can use. If they don't have resources like this, be the person who gets everyone in your group on board to use one.

MUSIC AND MOVIES
We are essentially little babies when it comes to learning languages. If we open our minds and stop resisting, like babies do, the language will just wash over us. Don't believe people who tell you language learning is hard! I mean, it is, but attitude is important. When babies are learning to speak or listening to people speak their home language, they spend a lot of time watching mouth movements, listening to music, looking at pictures, and identifying sounds. This is how they learn the language.

I particularly loved watching a Chinese adaptation of the Korean show "Running Man." I loved it because the actors in the show used simple language and repeated it episode after episode. Be like a baby and learn like a baby. Listen to as many songs as you can and watch as many movies as you can. Before you know it, you will begin recognizing patterns of speech in the language, tones of voice, tones of words, and so on.

If you are struggling with studying a boring book, listening to music and watching movies is a great way to start your language learning before PST and continue your language learning after PST. You may not understand the language right away, but you will be able to look back and see how far you have come.

KEEP A JOURNAL

Tracking your progress is a good way to stay motivated with your language learning. A person is more likely to stay motivated when they see positive results. I remember the first Chinese character I drew without direction, and it looked like a 3-year-old wrote it when I checked back a few years later. You see this kind of behavior with people who lose a lot of weight. Same thing.

Keeping a journal where you can write stories, take notes, paste articles or anything in the host-country language, means that you can go back to your earlier entries and see how your grammar, vocab, and reading comprehension has improved.

Keeping a journal where you practice writing your language skills and the constant repetition of these practices can help you remember. After two years, you will be able to see the fruits of your practice.

Consider some of these methods, and if for some reason one of these doesn't work for you, there are other methods all over the internet that you can try. Look for your perfect fit and remember to consider your learning style. You can learn more about my Chinese Language Learning methods at TravelBranyik.com.

As you start learning the language and taking your courses, take a moment to do this exercise below. You will want to keep good track of your goals for language learning and how you are progressing and reaching those goals! Answer these questions below to decide where you want to be with you language.

- What are your goals for language learning?
- How will you measure your progress?
- What tools will you use to help you learn?
- Where do you see your language level in 6 months? 12 months?
- Do you have a long-term goal with your language and what is it?
- How can you use this language in the future or in your career?

NEW VOLUNTEER, NEW SITE, NEW EXPERIENCE

I SAT IN THE MIDDLE OF THE ROOM in a chair. A silent nervousness hung in the air as a small group of Peace Corps Chinese staff sat around me on the inside of the room. The white and Pepto pink walls were dirtied, and you could see places where students had written on them. There appeared to be a small peephole in the wall behind one of the staff, where the students could pass notes I assumed. I was surrounded by the pressure to perform well and by the people who would ultimately decide where I would serve in China.

For the next twenty minutes, or however long it was, I can't remember, I talked about myself, my desires, my skills, my strengths, my weaknesses, and my English abilities. I also told them where I wanted to live in China. They looked at me, studying me, taking notes, and asking questions. Before I knew it, before I could realize I had been through the interview, it was over. For the next week or so, I carried uncertainty of where I would soon live in China.

In my head, I thought of the four provinces of China that volunteers worked in. When the staff told us about the provinces, they showed pictures corresponding with each province, Sichuan, Guizhou, Gansu, and Chongqing. The only picture that I could remember was the Chongqing photo. It was just a photo of high rise buildings in what looked like an industrial zone. There was no trace of the sky, mountains, trees, or even people. I only saw heavy smog in the background. I immediately noted to myself how much I didn't want to live in Chongqing.

After that week or so of worry, the anticipation of our coming site placement seemed to be on everyone's mind. On a rainy Friday in Chengdu, all volunteers were bussed from their training sites and homestay families to the Peace Corps headquarters for site placements announcements, otherwise known as the place we would be living and serving over the next two years. We were alive with excitement so early in the morning. As soon as we entered the large brightly lit conference room, there were whoops and cheers from the volunteers all eager to begin site placements.

The country director announced each volunteer's site placement one by one. Each volunteer ran to the front of the conference room to take hold of their special colored envelope corresponding with their province. Blue for Gansu, pink for Sichuan, green for Guizhou, and yellow for Chongqing.

We were told that inside each envelope would be information about our school – phone numbers, counterparts' names, programs, campus size, and location – along with a site guide from the volunteer who previously served at the site.

I waited, for what seemed like forever, watching each volunteer bound from chair to envelope and return to their provincial group with excitement. When I heard my name, I walked to the front, and a yellow envelope was placed in my hand. I felt sick and sad.

Being from a small Colorado town, I didn't want to go to this province to begin with because of the large city feel and lack of nature. I walked to the Chongqing group in a mope, reading the front cover where the name of my school was written boldly: Chongqing Vocational Tourism School.

I unbuttoned the thin, plastic, yellow envelope to explore the information that would soon be my next home. I pulled out one thin packet of paper stapled together and began reading about my school. This packet was the only thing inside the envelope. There was no site guide from a volunteer. *GULP*

Not long after all site placements were announced, I was approached by Sandy Peng, the program manager for all Chongqing volunteers. She excitedly told me that this was a brand-new site and

I would be the first volunteer ever to teach there. She raved on about the many opportunities that come with being a new volunteer and how I would forever be remembered for setting the Peace Corps foundation. Then she told me I would be teaching in a high school.

double GULP

Peace Corps China normally serves in Colleges and Universities. Mrs. Peng was very excited that I was given this opportunity and she continued talking about how perfect I was for this site. I'm sure my face held no excitement. During my generation of volunteers, there was only a handful of others working in vocational high schools and two other volunteers working in a middle school. Everyone else would be working in a university or college with higher level students.

I tried for a while to be optimistic and see the upsides of this new coming experience, trying hard to digest Sandy's promises of a great opportunity. I watched others around me who seemed to be very confident. And why wouldn't they be? They were stepping into a school that had generations of PCVs before them, a general support system, and they had an office of supervisors who knew how to care for an expat. Regardless, I tried to think of this like it was going to be a normal PC experience, but I didn't consider a few things, nor had I been aware of the challenges ahead.

New site means new hurdles and basically a new everything. Because this site was new, they didn't have the experience of working with Peace Corps or even hosting a foreign teacher. Both the host school and volunteer were unlikely to have a cross-cultural experience. Needless to say, it would be a learning experience for everyone. This also meant there was bound to be miscommunication and misunderstanding around the role of the volunteer within the school, which meant a lot of things not explained and a lot of things lost in translation. This meant both the school and I would no doubt have many new firsts as we tried to make these two years work well.

There was a lot I would have to figure out on my own, something other volunteers never had to face after being part of a school with active PCVs for over a decade. It wasn't until after I began work at my new site I figured something out. The TEFL training we were given during PST, which is geared toward college level, did not support my efforts working in a high school. I also didn't know this was a vocational tourism high school and that I would be working with extremely low-level students who couldn't speak let alone understand English. In addition to this, I had no teaching or language skills, which made this job much more difficult than I ever expected. I still never figured out why I was at Chongqing Tourism School and even after my service, I never understood why Sandy picked me.

I didn't know being a volunteer to open a new site was even a possibility within Peace Corps or that this kind of situation could happen to a volunteer.

Most daunting was my lack of skills for such a crucial position. And it was a crucial position. Being the first PCV to open a new site is a lot of work, there is a significant amount of pressure to perform well and a great desire to not let my counterparts or Peace Corps down. It takes a lot of patience, a lot of understanding, and an incredible amount of communication.

I spent a lot of time expressing my thoughts and struggles about time in the classroom with my students, brainstorming ways to engage them, brainstorming ways to collaborate with my colleagues, and still, after two years, I never found an effective way to teach students that catered to their needs and interests. Such a unique experience like this was difficult to explain to my Chinese counterparts in a way they could understand, relate to, or care about. But it was very new for them too.

There were many times I went home and cried because I couldn't believe this was my service.

I had imagined something totally different – teaching literature at a university and my students falling in love with me. I imagined traveling to new places, seeing new things, and the ease of meeting new people. But that didn't happen. This phase of my life changed me in so many ways. It was okay that it wasn't what I expected.

I showed up to my first day of oral English class with my first-year students in the sweltering heat of late August. I walked to my first class of students who were whispering about the new volunteer. Upon entering the room, I was met with applause and excitement. I thought to myself, this won't be so bad at all. I spoke a joyful and well enunciated, 'Hi' to the class, who replied likewise in unison. I wrote my name on the board and introduced myself.

Shortly after, I handed out fifty syllabi to the students in my class, I opened my mouth to speak English and jaws dropped. Not a single student knew what I was saying. I held tight to the well thought out, dense, unbelievably organized syllabus in my hand, sweat drenching my palms and continued painfully going over the syllabus in English. Students were staring at me in disbelief, some started playing with their phones, and when it came time to engage them, I received no response. I was relieved when the bell rang and I could leave the uncomfortable classroom atmosphere. After walking out of the class, I threw out the syllabus I had worked diligently on and tried to go back to my office without crying.

I was at a loss for what to do next. If only I had taken my parents advice. If only I the attitude of, "What an opportunity this is!" But I was afraid. It took me a while to take their advice.

The experience became so upsetting, I knew I had to do something positive before I did something as drastic as quitting. While it seemed the school wasn't what I dreamed, my school happened to be located in a part of the city that was incredibly convenient and magical compared to a lot of other sites. My apartment was newly remodeled and furnished, it was situated right beside the light rail, and was within a five-minute walk from Walmart, H&M, Starbucks, and a few gyms.

At the time, I was 50 pounds overweight and had a habit of getting lost in incredibly unhealthy coping mechanisms. But I had made a promise to myself, before joining Peace Corps that I would find a healthier method of coping. So, the 5'4", 190-pound little me, joined a gym.

People will say how great their service was because of their interaction with the school, but the reason my service was great was that of my interaction with the community. After joining the gym, I started leading a healthier lifestyle, losing 50 pounds in two years, and I made friends with locals. Most all of my friends barely spoke English and so with great desire to better my relationships I started studying Chinese, knowing that bettering these skills meant making more friends. My Chinese went from good to great! I could communicate in the classroom with my low-level English learners, even to the level of being able to discipline. Language became my pathway to greatness, to grow.

Despite my major improvements in the language and my ability to communicate with my students and my community, there was still a lot I was failing at. Every term, I changed my lesson plans and semester plans in attempts to find a new method for teaching teenagers who cared very little about learning English. And with each year, my English corner had failed, and my Secondary Project of trying to develop an English Corner effectively had also failed.

The first term with Chongqing Tourism School was basically me, stumbling around, trying to find my feet, letting the students have their way and feeling totally incompetent. The second term, I learned from my mistakes, stopped letting the students push me around and started disciplining them more through instilling classroom rules and cell phone policies – I was working with teenagers, some may know what that's like. By the third term, I settled into the idea that maybe there wasn't much I could do to make this work. I started doing my best, getting to know my students, and trying to find ways to get to the students who really did care.

By the fourth term, I decided that if I was going to teach anything to my kids, any one thing, it would be the phrase, "Can I go to the bathroom?"

Worked like a charm.

I felt no remorse or sadness in leaving the school after my Close of Service (COS), it had been taxing for the entire two years. I felt great relief knowing my teaching would be over soon, but even so, I was sad about leaving China. Before my COS, I questioned if having a second volunteer in this school would be beneficial since I felt I had done so little. I hadn't developed secondary projects, and I felt I hadn't gotten exactly what I wanted out of my service within the school. And yet, I was excited to pass on what I had learned to the next volunteer with hopes they could be the difference in the school I felt I wasn't.

In my last week of teaching, two of the seven classes of students I taught, presented me with gifts and good tidings as I made my way out of service. Both classes presented me with a jar filled to the brim with flowers and messages written in English and Chinese thanking me and wishing me the best in life. I remember one of them reading, "You are my angel." One by one, the children met me at the front of the classroom to give me a hug -- hugs are not customary in China but are meant to show great affection. It seemed I had not failed as much as I thought I did and perhaps in some small form, I had reached my students, even if they had never said it out loud.

I spent the last few weeks at my site in Chongqing, eating my favorite food, hanging out with my friends, going to the gym, and thinking about just how much this experience had changed me. Maybe I hadn't been the change I wanted to see in the school, maybe I didn't create as many friendships as I thought, and maybe the school will remember our experience as challenging and upsetting.

I will remember I didn't know Chinese before this. I found the will to be patient with myself. I learned how to communicate better. I learned how to let go of what I couldn't control. I learned how to stay strong and power through, and above all, I didn't quit. The experience of being a new volunteer at a new site humbled me, it changed the way I looked at the world, how I thought about people, and it broadened my compassion for people's situations. Peace Corps did that for me and ultimately gave me a sense of accomplishment. Looking back at the difficulties and struggles, I would do it all again, and the exact same way.

During my last month with Peace Corps, Sandy came to visit my school and my counterparts. She told me my school would be inviting another volunteer to replace me once I was gone. "Generally, if a new volunteer has successfully completed two years at a new site, this means the site can continue the program successfully! I am proud of you." She said to me. I was shocked this was a truth, and I may have been instrumental in continuing this program. Then sadly, over a month after my COS, Sandy told me they would not be sending a PCV to my school for reasons unknown.

Peace Corps is always doing their best to extend the program to new places so we can continue to make a positive difference in the world. While my story is a unique and specific situation, it happens with a very small fraction of volunteers. I wanted to share this story to bring awareness to all volunteers, letting them know that this is and can be a possibility for you if you join Peace Corps. This can also be an experience where you don't know what you are doing. But if this does happen, you have the strength to power through, we all do, with anything.

Although I struggled and my projects fell through, my experience could help another volunteer have a revolutionary experience developing a new program or project that benefits the community. There are endless possibilities. Be open to all of them, buck up, and make the most of the situation.

WORKING WITH HOST COUNTRY COUNTERPARTS

WHEN I ARRIVED in Chongqing at the train station to meet with my counterparts, there was a lot of silence between us. It was enough awkwardness to make me want to go back to the U.S. and be where everything was comfortable. During our cross-cultural training, we learned a lot about the differences between American habits, mannerisms, emotions, etc. and I knew I would be different. The tension and stress of dealing with people in a country that is the polar opposite of you can be terrifying. And it was terrifying for the first few weeks.

Thankfully, my counterpart was great, and we built a friendship that will last forever.

Learning how to work well with your counterparts and Host HCNs will have a lot to do with the Second Goal of your service, "helping promote a better understanding of Americans on the part of the peoples served."

I was the type of person who wasn't afraid to express emotions when I needed to. I was very open. Chinese people are much more reserved and spend less time complaining or sharing their emotions and internal struggles. It took a lot of time for me to adapt. I was humbled by this.

54

I recognized I spent more time talking about myself or complaining about something that didn't matter rather than shifting my attitude toward something more constructive or positive. To this day, I feel embarrassed at the times when that emotional part of me came out. I'm sure it made my supervisors and counterparts uncomfortable.

For us to work well together, there needed to be a lot of adaptation for both myself and the people I was working with. I understood that my situation at this school as the first foreign teacher would be delicate and would require a tremendous amount of patience.

Both my host school and I didn't really know what to expect, and there would be plenty of learning opportunities. During one of our first meetings, I told them, "I want us to communicate everything with transparency in every situation. If I do something wrong, please tell me, and I will do the same for all of you."

Fortunately, my primary counterpart, Erin, had lived in the United States for five years to attend Michigan State University. She had some knowledge of what Americans were like, and it was easy to confide in her.

There are a few things I think are essential for working with your counterparts effectively. I learned through trial and error, and the more I got to know people.

HAVE PATIENCE
You are heading into cultures you may not know and learning languages you never knew existed. If this makes you anxious, relax. It takes time to

develop these skills and knowledge. By the end of your service, you may still feel like you're not finished learning. When you are adjusting to life at site, life teaching, life integrating and then you add the extra tasks of learning language and culture, it's easy to lose your patience.

There are many ways to counter these kinds of feelings. Rather than losing your patience, take a few moments to find your happy place and recollect yourself. Go somewhere quiet or somewhere you feel safe if you need to. Remind yourself you are a baby at this point. I mean that in a constructive way.

You are like a new baby learning to speak, learning from the experienced and there are very few lucky enough to already know the drill. You are allowed to stumble around, fall over, get back up and keep walking. Peace Corps expects this to happen, and so does your host school. They have been well educated on the adaptation you undergo while you are finding your place in your school and community.

Work your ass off on a regular basis. If your colleagues see you are working diligently, contributing your time well, willing to adapt, and willing to learn, they are more likely to help you when you need it. This may take time, but I promise it will be worth it.

In addition to this, if you have issues with calming yourself instantaneously, pick up healthy habits to counter these feelings. If moments of impatience hit you during your office hours or downtime, practice meditation, journal your frustrations, talk to a loved one back home, talk to a colleague or friend in your community you can trust and ask for advice, or exercise. There are numerous ways to calm feelings of impatience and distress.

SPEND TIME LEARNING THE CULTURE/LANGUAGE
There is a bit of a disadvantage of joining Peace Corps without prior knowledge, skills or understanding in the culture or language. I spent a lot of time learning both. Once I immersed myself in learning the language, I was amazed at how much easier everything was for me and my relationships with my colleagues, students, and friends. I was always in motion when it came to learning about China and learning Mandarin. This contributed to my success in the end.

Because I didn't have prior knowledge, it took a while for me to feel comfortable around people, understand people, socialize effectively, say all the right things, be respectful in customary ways, you get the idea. There was nothing I could do to control this learning curve. It just took time.

Some volunteers don't experience this at all. Some don't learn the language and still have incredibly strong relationships. It depends! Some Peace Corps countries have been hosting volunteers for so long they know how diverse we are. It means they have an incredible amount of patience, compassion, and willingness to be there if for some reason you fall.

When you learn about all the corners of the culture, you'll also learn helpful rules and techniques to display your feelings of respect to a person. My counterpart, Erin, is a very caring and attentive person. She was great at listening to me when I was upset, great at giving me advice, and she showed her care and respect for me by doing simple things. She brought me fruit, brought me souvenirs when she went on trips or invited me to her home for dinner. These behaviors are so common in Chinese culture that I became a copycat. I observed the way she showed her affection and practiced the same behavior, giving fruits to my colleagues, and even little notes. Simple things like this contributed to building relationships and building a good reputation for me.

It depends on each culture. Maybe giving fruit is customary in China, but not somewhere else in the world. But hey, the best thing to do it always ask your colleagues and friends. Showing your interest in understanding these rules is also a great contributor to building relationships. It tells your colleagues you care and you are making an effort.

I'm telling you to spend time learning the culture and language because I believe it contributes in huge ways to keeping healthier relationships within your school and community. The positive relationships you create in your community during service may set the pace for the next volunteer coming to take your place and carry on the legacy. Keep that in mind.

PRACTICE COMMUNICATION
I said before that I felt communication was so important. It was a very big problem for me in my school during my service despite my efforts to encourage transparency. In my school, there were times the staff overlooked giving me information about school events, schedule changes, school policies or expectations, and knowledge about how to effectively teach the children.

It was so aggravating, but it wasn't their fault. We were all working with what we knew. Over time it got better. I made a point to communicate my concerns to my Peace Corps staff so they could talk to my school about how I felt. It was important for me to ensure my counterparts weren't embarrassed while we were all on the learning curve. We were all on this journey together.

I never stopped communicating just because I was tired or I felt like I wasn't being heard. I shared my ideas and concerns often. I really wanted to create this bubble where my colleagues found me approachable. If they could approach me, I knew it would be easier to get collaboration on projects, assistance when teaching the children, etc.

Being the first volunteer at my school, I really wanted to pave the way for communication. I wanted all of my colleagues and students to feel comfortable talking to me without fear of rejection or embarrassment so that when the next volunteer arrived, they had a hell of a lot easier time talking with their colleagues when they needed to. I really wanted the next volunteer to feel comfortable when they joined the team.

LET GO OF EGO

The "this is how we do it in America" attitude is probably by far the most damaging attitude toward building relationships with your colleagues in Peace Corps. I had this attitude at the beginning.

At first, when I would say things of that nature, I almost equated it to teaching American culture. What it came off as was, "This is what your country is doing wrong." It was pretentious, condescending, and disrespectful. It didn't take long for me to shed this mentality, but it got so bad at times my own counterparts were afraid to approach me to tell me how they felt. That is not what I wanted, especially since I was clear about building communication between us.

If a person sees their way as being the only right way, it can damage relationships as well as the host school's perception of Americans in general. As shallow as that is, it is the truth. Your one experience with a person in your host country could forever reflect their opinion of you and other Americans. That gossip will spread like wildfire.

Let the EGO go. It's more important to discuss different views in constructive ways than suggest your way is the right one. This attitude will not build relationships. You'll make more friends if you can learn to set your EGO free.

If you are having struggles with your counterpart, contact your Peace Corps Staff. But if you have done all you can and things still have not progressed, try this exercise below to encourage positive thinking.

Get out a piece of paper or a journal. Right now, you may be going through every flaw you see in your counterpart. Let's recognize the good in them.

- Write between five and ten positive qualities you see in your counterpart.
- After you have written these, recall a time that your counterpart did something nice for you or someone else you know.
- List 1-2 ways you could encourage a bonding moment with them (lunch, coffee, tea, a walk outside, etc.)

Understanding you community doesn't have to be difficult. As Americans, we have a tendency to do things on our own because most likely, we were raised to be independent adults. It's our way and there is nothing wrong with our way. But as you join the Peace Corps, you need to find a healthy even ground between what you were raised knowing and feeling and what you are learn to adapt to in your country of service.

To speak more to this, below is a story about Jenna, who learned how to belong to the village of Tsarasambo in Madagascar.

When I was 25 years old, I took a gigantic step towards adulthood: I moved into my first house! Well, it was a hut made of sticks. And I guess I wasn't fully embracing adulthood because there would be no gas, water, or electric bills to pay – seeing as I would have none of those amenities– but it was still my house! My first home.

As the hot season on the East Coast of Madagascar simmered away, I slowly became more and more settled in the quiet village of Tsarasambo, where I was now serving as a Peace Corps Volunteer. Each day my joyful neighbors would stop by my house offering to help me with things: fetching water, washing my clothes, cooking rice, or cleaning my yard.

It was truly kind of them to offer, but I was having trouble accepting such kindness. I wanted to take care of things myself! I was used to the individualistic mind set of an American. There had to be an angle. If they wanted to help, they must surely expect something in return? And how does one work out a payment system with their neighbors? I had two years ahead of me. I wanted to be careful with my relationships.

After a few months, I decided to plant a garden in my yard. I bought a shovel and began to dig a hole. Just minutes later, after standing in the hot sun and pretending I knew what I was doing, a group of neighborhood children flocked to my house, tore the shovel from my hands, and began digging the hole for me. Ah crap! I thought, the Peace Corps Policy Handbook clearly states that child labor is unacceptable...

With no physical effort exerted on my part, a large hole soon appeared next to my house. Peace Corps had been pushing the idea of "Double Digging" so the hole was about 42 centimeters. It was wide and alarmingly deep!

The hole sat there for a while. I didn't know what to do with it. To be honest, I didn't know the first thing about gardening and I was afraid of starting just to watch everything die right before my eyes. A few weeks later there was still an untouched pit in my yard. It became a joke. Independence Day was coming up and one of the men from an NGO I was working with said that if anyone gets too drunk or out of control, they would be disposed of in the hole.

As warmer weather returned and the possibility of rain lessened, I continued to let the hole for my garden wither away, covered in dust and overgrown weeds.

A year passed. Due to heavy winds dismantling the fence around my house and neglect on my part, it truly looked like a cyclone had hit my yard. On the East Coast of Madagascar, it would be totally realistic to say that a cyclone had hit my yard, but it had been an El Niño year and there had been no serious cyclones. Good for the community of course, but bad for my excuse as to why my house looked terrible.

It was time for me to do something. I'd lived in the village community for over a year at that point. Despite the hideous and neglected appearance of my house, I had come to understand Malagasy culture better. I had developed strong relationships with my neighbors. As Mother Nature had slowly chipped away at my yard, my stubbornness to do things on my own had slowly chipped away as well.

I was living in a Collective Society. There was no such thing as "individualism." I was already weird enough for looking different, sounding different, and living alone, there was no need to make myself look even crazier by refusing assistance. In a village everyone helps each other... for the sake of helping. That's it. No matter how much I wanted to stand alone, the village wanted to support me and help me to stand straighter. I'd relented. I hadn't fetched my own water in months. There was nothing I could do to stop it. People would bring me fruit and if I did not like the fruit, I would simply pass it on to someone else. If I had leftover food I would give it to my neighbor. If I ever had a problem, there were many people I could ask for help, and they would jump up and accomplish the task with exuberance. Everything I did was intertwined with support from the community in which I lived. I was growing to fit the village.

I asked the people at the mayor's office if they could fix my fence. I received surprised laughter when I told them "tsy bogosy tranoko." My house is not handsome. Sure enough, after a few weeks of "Fotoana-gasy" Malagasy time, a new fence was gradually erected around my house.

So I had a fence. Now it was time to attempt to make a garden again. I told some of my neighbors and people I worked with in the community about my plan. The following day, everyone I knew stormed my yard and began tearing things apart. Moms with babies on their backs were digging up weeds. Teenagers were hacking away at invasive plants. Kids were sweeping up the discarded bushes and sticks.

Once my yard looked nicely shaven, some of the women I'd worked with throughout the year arrived with plants, flowers, and cow poop for fertilizer. They chopped up some dirt and began placing the greenery around my house. Things were starting to look snazzy.

This was the day that I realized my house was not my house.

The following week, everyone returned to help me plant a vegetable garden. I had another Peace Corps Volunteer come to help, though I admit she was there mainly just to motivate me.

The children already knew how to plant everything. Tomatoes, beans, corn, peanuts, zucchini. They wouldn't let me help. Fine. They didn't need me.

Each day that followed, children would scour the garden, looking for what had already begun to grow. There were three different groups of children that would take turns fetching water and sprinkling the plants throughout the day.

Every morning at 5 am without fail, I could hear my neighbor, a sweet mother of four who'd claimed me as another of her children, walking around and watering everything.

My house was not my house. My yard was not my yard. My garden was not my garden. It was everyone's house. It was everyone's yard. It was everyone's garden. It all belonged to the village of Tsarasambo.

I belonged to the village of Tsarasambo.

Jenna Smith
Madagascar '15 –'17

SERVICE STRUGGLES AND HEALTHY COPING MECHANISMS

WHEN YOU START Peace Corps and go through orientation, the Peace Corps Medical Staff will show you this fun little flow chart dictating your emotions for the next two years. It shows the honeymoon phases and phases of depression you are likely to experiences during Peace Corps.

I resisted this idea. I thought to myself, why am I already being condemned to periods of sadness when I haven't even experienced anything yet? The truth, most of us will go through these periods of total happiness and total depression because we believe they will happen. That doesn't have to be all of us.

Some volunteers make the most of their service because they had the right attitude. Those volunteers are the greatest teachers. I asked them for advice often. Other people (myself included) make mountains out of molehills. Eventually, they find solace and usually not long after constructing their mountains. We'll get to that story in a bit.

I would like to propose an idea to you at this moment. When you see this flowchart, pretend it doesn't exist. Challenge yourself to create your own flow chart! It can be easy to listen to the medical officers and the dreaded flowchart and then make excuses for the moments when you are sad and upset – whether it be because you are homesick, you are having a rough day with Peace Corps, or you are struggling with the culture.

Look at each moment you experience as a learning opportunity. After I taught my first day of class and realized my students had a very low English level, I went home, bawled my eyes out, and questioned if I was even capable of doing this. I thought maybe this was the point where I went home, where I would quit and go back to doing what was easy. I spent a lot of my time in China feeling upset about things that didn't go my way or things weren't living up to my expectations. But there were times I also took a situation of hardship and decided to overcome it by learning from it or changing how I felt by doing something positive.

When I couldn't speak the language with my students to help them learn, I only sat around for a short time complaining about it. I decided to go and do something about it. I involved myself in the language, learned a little each day, and before I knew it, I was using both Chinese and English to teach in the classroom. I could connect with my students better. Instead of just quitting, or wallowing in the fact that I couldn't communicate, I came up with a solution and I made an active effort to change my situation. I failed three terms in a row, but I made an effort. You have to keep on.

I experienced a difficult Peace Corps service. I was afraid of what would happen. I was afraid of being homesick. I was afraid no one understood me. I had carved out expectations of what my life would be like in China, but none of them were that positive. Looking back on it now, I recognize I had the wrong attitude during my service, even though I thought the flow chart was bogus. There were a lot of times I was a sad excuse for a person, but I was learning and changing. My growth depended on me. I know if I had tackled life in China with a different attitude, I would've had a more positive lifestyle there. However, I learned some great lessons about myself, changed a lot of selfish perceptions, and grew in unimaginable ways. This could happen to you too. Focus on staying positive always.

It can be difficult to remove ourselves from those moments when we feel helpless. It may seem easier to sit in self-pity, homesickness, binge-watching movies, eating comfort food, drinking, or sleeping all day.

It can be challenging to get out of these moments, but you must do it. You must get up. You must make friends. You need to be outside. You need to find your center. You need to live the vision you dreamt up of Peace Corps. You need to live life and realize you signed up for this and it's your great opportunity to be where you are!

This next portion is personal advice on how to cope with moments of distress. This could involve something, anything that lights up your heart and helps you achieve the goals you came to carry out during your service. I am hoping you refer to this part of the book to help you get through the rough days. If you take anything from what I've shared, let it be the contents of this chapter: Meditation, Gratitude Journal, Exercise, Relying on PCV's, Relying on Peace Corps Staff, Relying on Community, and Travel.

MEDITATION
Having a rough day? Take ten minutes. Ten minutes to sit down and meditate. Meditation works wonders in bringing you back to your center. I like to use the Headspace app. It's free, it doesn't demand a lot of your time, and it teaches you to clear your mind and breathe through your situations. Headspace even applauds you when you have meditated every day.

By meditating each day, you are choosing to be chill, stay centered, and have a positive attitude. Optimistic attitudes can lead to positive moments and experiences throughout your day. Even a few deep breaths help.

GRATITUDE JOURNAL
I know this seems strange, but I swear it works wonders. There was a time I was very frustrated with my teaching situation and my ability to communicate with my students. Wrap that up with my moments of being homesick, or feeling isolated, and I was looking for another reason to go home. Instead, I started a 30-Day Gratitude Journal which you can read more about on TravelBranyik.com.

For 30 consecutive days straight, I committed to writing about the good things that happened and the things I wanted to happen for me tomorrow. By writing down the positive, I focused less on the negative and put out more positive vibes for days to come. Bring a notebook or journal, colored pencils, and pens. Write, draw, and envision what you want your experience to be. The more optimism you put into your experience, the more optimism you will get out of it.

EXERCISE

I used exercise as my center point for feeling better about my situation. Luckily, I was able to go exercise at a local gym. If I had a rough day teaching, I could go work the punching bag. If I was homesick, I could go for a 30 minutes run on the treadmill. If I just wanted to feel like a badass, I would go lift weights or do High- Intensity Interval Training (HIIT). Exercise is the reason I made it through my Peace Corps service. I also lost a ton of weight and felt even better about myself.

When you exercise your body releases endorphins, and when you release endorphins, you feel happy. So, exercise! For your health and happiness. Committing to at least 30 minutes of exercise at least five times a week can work wonders for you. Whether you like yoga, taking a long run, doing bodyweight exercises, or doing HIIT, it doesn't matter, as long as you do something! You'll feel better on those rough days.

RELY ON OTHER PCVS

You will undoubtedly build camaraderie while you're in service. The people you build bonds with will be life-long friends.

I was fortunate enough to live in the same province as a very dear friend of mine, Damien Shuck. We were both from Colorado and would reminisce about our home and the foods we missed. Damien is a character, and he was constantly finding ways to make me laugh. He was also a great listener. When I was upset, I would call, he would listen, then he would make jokes, and I would be laughing again. Whenever we needed a friend or needed someone to talk to, we could rely on each other. And, added bonus, whenever we got together, we indulged in some food therapy by making some of our favorite Mexican dishes!

If I ever felt upset, isolated or helpless, Damien was my go to and 95% of the time, he made me feel better. You will have these people, and if they are good people (which I'm sure they will be), you can have faith that they will raise you up and help you see the bigger picture.

It also helps to call home using FaceTime or other video chat programs and apps. I utilized the FaceTime option regularly to call those who understood me best, my parents.

RELY ON PEACE CORPS STAFF
I had an amazing Program Manager named Sandy. She chose me for one of the most difficult and rewarding lessons of my life. She was incredibly supportive of me. Whenever I needed her, she was there. I could call her or email her to talk about something that was bothering me. I called her to tell her when something amazing happened. Sometimes, she would drop by, and we would have a few moments to eat lunch and chat. She was one of those people who believed in me when I didn't believe in myself.

All flowcharts aside, the Peace Corps staff is looking out for you. They will do whatever they can to help you feel comfortable, happy, and safe during your service. Remember they have seen many different situations of hardship among the volunteers. They will know how to comfort you.

Schedule lunch with your Peace Corps Staff members, take your Program Manager out to coffee or send a simple email to any PC staff member you trust to ask them for advice. There is untold value in building these relationships.

RELY ON YOUR COMMUNITY
My counterpart Erin became my best friend when I was living in Chongqing. Whenever she knew I was having a rough time, she would invite me over to have dinner with her family, or she would invite me to a hot pot date! (Learn more about hot pot and Chinese cuisine at TravelBranyik.com). She was always there for me on my worst days and made me laugh. Erin had lived in America for five years so she could relate to what I was going through, which made things so much easier for me.

You have counterparts and community members who care about you and want to spend time with you. Those moments of delight can be shared with the owner of your local restaurant or the ladies and gentlemen at your supermarket, someone you pass on the street, or a friend from the nearby gym. It can be anybody. Chances are, they already know you and want to chat. It may just be the lifting up you need to realize that you are living a life most people dream of! You are creating memories for yourself and leaving marks on everyone you meet. What a great feeling that is!

TRAVEL

Oh my gosh, if you are abroad, you better damn well be traveling. If you're in Madagascar, you should be riding bicycles down dirt roads and in between those crazy beautiful Baobab trees. Peace Corps gives you a certain amount of days out of the year to vacation, but don't forget those short weekend trips you can take to a nearby town or city to see something incredible.

I once took a weekend trip to Hainan Province, which is coined "the Hawaii of China." I spent two days walking along the beaches barefoot and I got to see the Goddess of Mercy on the Edge of the World. It was breathtaking. It was a destination I dreamt of visiting before I came to China. I was in happy tears when I finally realized a dream destination of mine had come true. Nothing lifts your spirits like fulfilling promises you made to yourself.

It helps to get away from your site and see something different. We can get stuck in the routine and forget to give ourselves the time we need to replenish those feel-good emotions we need to function. Taking a short trip to a town you want to go to or even taking a day trip to a local coffee shop or ancient town can be enough. Do whatever speaks to you and your passions!

There are plenty of great opportunities to turn your day from good to great. At the end of the day, you will have the choice to be happy or sad. You have complete power over making the most of any situation. Define your Peace Corps experience as being totally kick ass, rather than a series of sad stories.

If your rough day of service has brought you to read through this portion, then practice the exercise below.

Write down everything positive that happened for you this week.

- Take a few moments to plan a short weekend trip for yourself and then carry out the adventure!
- Write down the names of five people in your life you are thankful for and why.
- Envision a recent moment when you felt happy. Recall the feelings, smells, tastes, and other sensations
- Make a short list of goals you hope to accomplish while you are still in service.

"Give yourself a little bit of grace," as my friend Teresa would say.

We've covered a lot! Let's end with a beautiful story from an RPCV who served in Samoa. Her story is a beautiful example of finding solutions and the healing powers of water.

The first time my water went out, it was a fairly simple fix. It happened first thing in the morning as I attempted to go about my usual routine of brushing my teeth and washing my face. I turned the faucet on the sink to discover the small trickle of water that had been steadily dwindling over the past few days had disappeared altogether. I felt utterly betrayed and confused. The possibility had never occurred to me that I might one day turn on a sink and water would not flow. Betrayal and confusion gave way to frustration at being stuck with morning breath, despair at yet one more thing having gone wrong, and a crushing sense of powerlessness because the universe was clearly out to get me. I sulked for a few hours while the village woke up, realized the universe was not actually out to get me and decided to take action. I asked around to figure out who the village plumber was, and once I found him he genially agreed to come look at my pipes. The pipes to my sink ran along the back wall outside my house, and after giving them a good shake, water once again ran smoothly from the sink. Voila!

The second time my water went out, it was not a simple fix. Having learned the secret ways of the plumber, I knew that I only needed to give the pipes a good shake in order to have this elixir of life restored to nourish my daily activities. I walked around back, gave the pipes a good shake, and returned to the bathroom to relish the fruits of my labor. Nothing. I tried again, shaking somewhat more vigorously than the first attempt. Still nothing. My sink had stopped flowing.

Lack of running water had a much broader impact on my life than I could have ever predicted. It affected my ability to make meals, drink tea, wash dishes, do laundry, and keep myself and my house clean. These immediate impacts also led to secondary impacts. I stopped running for a while due to complications with laundry and trying to keep my hair clean. Sweaty clothes very quickly became moldy clothes if not taken care of in a timely fashion. That was a short-term impact, though, as I soon realized not running was a greater threat to my sanity and well-being than running and facing the possibility of moldy clothes.

Each difficulty eventually resolved itself into an acceptable solution. After large rainstorms, I sometimes woke up in the cool of the night to hear the faucets flowing, leading to 3 am laundry sessions completed by the light of a headlamp on a few lucky occasions. I gratefully accepted offers of meals and beverages from people in the village without any question as to whether it had been prepared according to official Peace Corps recommendations. My life developed a new and different homeostasis. This unexpected change even brought moments of joy. When I was unable to do laundry at home, I made my way down to the small waterfall at the end of the village early in the morning to beat both the heat and the crowds. With the shoreline in sight, I sat in solitude with the repetitive crash of the waves and settled into a meditative pattern of scrubbing and rinsing clothes. As the sun rose to light the day, tinting the endless horizon with fiery shades of pink and orange, my whole being accepted the world for exactly what it was and knew that everything was working out as intended, even with the drought.

Natalie Ziemba
Samoa '10 – '12

LGBTQI AND DIVERSITY

I GREW UP in Florence, Colorado, a wonderful, family place but slightly unfamiliar with diversity. They were defined as a more conservative community, and there was nothing wrong with that other than there was no encouragement to be different. It was several years before I met people unlike those I knew in my hometown.

I was a year into service with my fellow volunteers when I realized how amazing, supportive, and diverse our group really was. I had never experienced a group of people quite like mine. I am proud of all of them.

From the beginning, Peace Corps volunteers led many groups that encouraged unity for the LGBTQ volunteers and the volunteers of different ethnicities. During IST, groups presented their perspectives on living in China as someone of different sexual orientation and skin color. Through these groups, people could come together in a safe place and share their stories, triumphs, and difficulties living in China and serving as gay, lesbian, bisexual, transgender, queer, and racially different. I had never seen such unity in any other community I lived in, even college.

The two groups that stuck out with me the most were Peace Out! and Racially Similar, Racially Different (RSRD). Before I explain these groups and what they have done to provide support, I will tell you about how

71

China views people of different race, ethnicity, or sexual orientations.

If you are a person of white complexion in China, you are faced with attention daily. In China, people treat you as a novelty, and they enjoy the white foreigner spectacle. White skin is an attractive trait for the people in China. While people with white complexions view living in China as difficult, it is non-comparable to the experience people of darker complexions have. It is non-comparable to what other Asians experience. Every race and ethnicity experiences something different. So why does skin color matter?

In ancient Chinese culture, people of royalty would spend their day in palaces and out of the sun, meaning their skin was very fair. This was a desirable trait and symbolized wealth. If your skin was incredibly dark or tan, it implied that you worked in the fields, that you are a peasant, and that you are poor. Over time, this perspective stuck, and it carried on to the present day and became a form of discrimination. I was told my skin was so beautiful and women rushed to cover me with umbrellas so I wouldn't darken my skin while outside in the sun. When my Dominican Republic, Indian, African American, Mexican, Spanish, and Portuguese friends went out into public, they were observed more than I was, and sometimes more criticized.

With my Asians friends, the Chinese natives would inquire about them as if they were natives. They would assume they were born in China. In fact, they were so insistent that my friends often ended up arguing with the HCNs about their American heritage. The natives, who were in denial, would continue arguing with Asian volunteers without realizing they were insulting them. While you would think being Asian in China is easy, it may also be just as difficult.

I had gay and lesbian friends who couldn't confidently come out at their permanent sites because there was a possibility their colleagues, students, and community members would judge them. Many of these volunteers had come to terms with their sexual orientation for many years and remarked on having that "in the closet" feeling again after entering service.

But in some of the provinces, it was easier to express yourself and be who you were with minimal judgment from the community. It depends!

I'm not telling you this because you should be scared, or because you think you can change the culture and perspective. I am telling you this because

China has opinions of race, ethnicity, and sexual orientation. They have implications just as much as any other country of people. I'm telling you this so you can know and support your peers. I am telling you this so you can start to see race and sexual orientation in a different way. I am also telling you this so you know how you represent yourself, no matter what your race or sexual orientation. How you represent yourself can change someone's perspectives of you, your race, and your sexual orientation.

I knew a young woman in Peace Corps who lived in the same province as me. I would complain to her about how difficult it was to express my authentic self without being able to speak the language. She told me, "You do it through action, through kindness, and then before you know it, people will know you."

She came to stay with me for one weekend, and we decided to go out for lunch. We took the elevator down to the first floor, walked outside my building and as soon as we made it out the door, we ran into my neighbor and his 1-year-old grandson. They began speaking to me in Chinese, and the plump little Chinese baby giggled and smiled. We met for only a second before saying goodbye and going to lunch. My friend looked at me and she said, "You just did it. Showed who you are without really saying anything. That's how you connect with your community."

Who you are in character will have a lot more to do with how people view you than your sexual orientation or your skin color. It took my friend's kind words to help me understand this better. It also took the participation in the Peace Corps' volunteer-led groups to carry me that much further.

Peace Out! and Racially Similar, Racially Different were my two favorite groups because almost every single volunteer in both groups showed up to each training session to show support. I was astounded by the level of support people provided each other in these groups because it was unlike anything I had seen growing up.

PEACE OUT!
Peace Out! was a volunteer-created group focusing on the LGBTQ community. It was based out of Sichuan because Southern provinces like Sichuan were more open to the ideas of homosexuality. The group organized native Chinese speakers to come do talks for the volunteers and give their perspectives on being gay or lesbian in China.

Some of my favorite speakers were a couple from Taiwan. They had been together for several years, and they talked about how they overcame the criticisms of their orientation and their relationship. They also talked about being vegetarian. When the talk ended, they took questions from volunteers.

I remember a volunteer asking what the hardest part about being a same-sex couple in Asia was. Their response, "being vegetarian." The room erupted in laughter and I was in complete awe of them. They overcame everything and focused on what was most important, their love for each other.

Peace Out! also organized panels that offered several volunteers of different sexual orientations to give their individual perspectives. They sat them in the conference room, and their fellow volunteers would ask questions about their experiences being LGBTQ in China. They gave very clear perspectives and advice on how to serve as a volunteer while still being true to yourself. It was inspiring.

RACIALLY SIMILAR, RACIALLY DIFFERENT (RSRD)
Racially Similar, Racially Different (RSRD) was something that hit me the hardest. The group was organized in an effort to support all races. It focused on providing support to people of similar race and people of different race.

One of the most memorable sessions I attended for RSRD was the group acknowledgment. We came together in the second-floor conference room at the Kehuayuan Hotel in Chengdu, Sichuan.

There was one big circle of chairs and two inner circles of chairs. RSRD's presidents had organized PowerPoint slides that would prompt each group of different races to speak about their unique experiences defined by their skin color. Each group would have a chance to talk so everyone could share their stories and perspectives.

The center circle had the least number of chairs and was reserved for the people who would be confessing something regarding their perspective. The second circle was for people who wanted to confess something. The third circle was reserved for people who just wanted to listen.

For each slide focusing on each race, there were follow up questions. People passed the microphone around and told their stories, how they felt, what had affected them most, and how they overcame it.

Hearing the stories allowed me to see everyone on a completely different level. Most of the time, we are not able to relate to someone's experiences unless we are experiencing them ourselves or we know someone on a personal level.

Being a person who was different than everybody else in the country gave me a taste of what it might feel like to be someone who is not white and living in America. I could never match what I felt living in China, to what people have felt their whole lives in our own home country.

This was one of the best lessons I ever learned, and it changed me for the rest of my life. Living in China, and accepting the cultural differences was so difficult for me.

When I finally experienced the different perspectives of others, I was able to look at the Chinese culture and country as a whole and embrace it. I complained a little less and loved a little more. And it was because of this volunteer-led group, that I was able to experience this.

I was also able to release my own guilt about being colorblind and insensitive to other cultures and races. I also regarded myself as very accepting and compassionate, but I only knew how to do that to a certain extent because of where I grew up.

There are many other volunteer-led groups organized in many other countries of service that circle around race, ethnicity, gender, sex, and preference.

These groups vary and will depend on the country you serve in. Age can also be a huge part of diversity, whether you are younger or older, like our friend John below:

One of my first experiences in life as an adult was as a Peace Corps Volunteer to Iran (pronounced E-ron, not Aye-ran). I was 20 years old, just 2 years out of high school.

> *I was recruited by the Peace Corps because I had graduated from a technical institute with a degree in auto mechanics. At the time, Peace Corps was desperate to find vocational education teachers in various trades to teach in Iran's Industrial Arts programs in various high schools throughout the country.*

75

I was the youngest trainee, yet in our training group were many senior citizens. Most of the older ones were couples, retired welders, mechanics, carpenters and their wives. There were quite a few single guys and girls. We had a few librarians and a couple of musicians. We were a most diverse group! While serving in Iran, I met my future and current wife, who was recruited to work in a blood bank.

One of the couples was a recent college graduate in physical education and her husband, a cabinet maker in his late twenties. They had been married only a couple of years and were looking for adventure and hoping to get experience towards teaching credentials.

Another couple, a middle-aged sheet metal worker and his wife, who had been a homemaker, brought their 2 teenage sons.

One girl, a recent graduate from Julliard, played the flute and would end up in the Tehran symphony orchestra.

There were two librarians, one from the east coast and another from the west coast. They were both in their mid-twenties and looking to gain some work experience.

Another couple was a retired pipefitter and his wife. They had emigrated from Poland as a young couple and were well traveled. They were very friendly and outgoing; both were over 70 years of age. It felt like they were my grandparents!

Also in my training program were a couple of young mid-west farmers who were recent college graduates and thought they might prefer the Peace Corps to being drafted into the military.

Though not all of these people stayed the full two years, most did, and a few went on to serve a third year. I personally did 2 years in Iran and later served again in Tunisia.

John Gallo
Iran '70 – '72
Tunisia '76 – '78

Find these groups, or be responsible for spearheading them yourself depending on where you are in the world. They will provide you with so much love and support.

They will be there when you need them most, and they will provide opportunities for educating yourself, your community, and others. You will come home a changed person. I guarantee it.

Take a moment to reflect on your own perspective. Use your journal to reflect on your own race or sexual orientation.

- Do you see any challenges being present during your service?
- If you do, how do you think you will accomplish them?
- Who will you rely on?
- Challenge yourself to be open minded and look at the bigger picture with this exercise and then relax. You can make the most of your experience by being the beautifully unique person you are.

YOUR SECOND YEAR AND SECONDARY PROJECTS

ALL COUNTRIES ARE DIFFERENT, so the nature of your projects during your service depends on where you are placed. For China Volunteers, we are subject to a two-week teacher training during the summer. But for most other volunteers, a secondary project will be in order.

SECONDARY PROJECTS

A secondary project could be anything that your school needs that you can spearhead. Peace Corps will offer you the opportunities to write grants and utilize them to enhance an area in your school.

In my case, I added an English Corner, but it can be other things besides English Corner! It can be a book club, a library, a fitness program, a new method for obtaining water, or anything your community or school would need.

You can brainstorm different ideas before you get to your site, but then again, it depends on the year you're serving, the situation, and what moves you.

For secondary projects, it will be beneficial to talk with your school and community members about what they need. Keep in mind that sometimes, they may not know themselves. And because we are essentially a pair of outside eyes, we see things differently than those in the midst of it all.

Below is a story about how your projects and efforts can make a large impact on your community if you are starting small. Later, we will get to the nature of Summer Projects for you China-goers.

The real Return On Investment (ROI) of the Peace Corps is in the intangible, unquantifiable, and unknowable impacts that volunteers make. These impacts are made more often than not through the simplest acts. Sometimes, our inspirational actions are unconscious. Sometimes we are left feeling like there was no one watching. But always, we leave a ripple effect which can be felt for decades to come.

In this magic sauce of tiny Peace Corps Volunteer actions, sometimes a movement is born. Sometimes, the smallest idea and the most random observation can lead to meaningful change. So was the experience I had as a volunteer.

My original assignment was as a business developer with a community radio station in Talas, the western region of Kyrgyzstan. This flagship broadcasting center was well-resourced and well-established, with world-class training and a flow of European money to keep the gears greased. Their sustainability plan called for assisting other hopeful community radio stations around the country get started up and trained. This effort had been going on for a few years. The trainings were in full force, but the radio stations were slow to be built. Radio stations are technically complex, expensive, brick-and-mortar, physical construction projects. This is hard to make happen anywhere, especially in a place with limited resources.

One day, I came home to find my host mother sitting with other elders drinking tea. Not a rare occurrence, but something unexpected happened.

As I walked into the house, I was carrying my iPad in my hands. When I was called over to be introduced to the guests, the iPad was drawing everyone's attention.

One of the elder women grabbed it from me and looked at the blank, black screen. She saw the single button on the iPad and pressed it. The iPad came to life, and with a swipe, she was off to the races. She didn't understand English, but despite her lack of technical exposure and language comprehension, she was immediately swiping between pages, opening, and closing apps, and having a grand ole' time.

Now, to say that these elder women had no idea about technology would not be accurate. As a matter of fact, most Kyrgyz people have some sort of smartphone and

79

keep in touch with each other via Whatsapp, even the older generation. This got me thinking about the technichal problem of a radio station. Radio stations are hard to build. But a smartphone provides all the tools a journalist needs: camera, microphone, editing software, writing software, an internet connection, etc. And all this in an affordable, virus- free device which can last for hours without being connected to the power grid.

With this idea, I wrote a project plan to deploy smartphones to community journalists in 20 communities around the country. I shopped it to every embassy and NGO I could reach, and in the end, I found support from the United Nations and the European Union Commission. They initially signed on to support the project for three years, via a local journalism school that I identified as the local partner.

4 years later, KyrgyzMedia.com is a fully sustainable news site, focusing exclusively on events taking place in rural areas of the country. This community of journalists is reaching followers all around the world and are broadcasting information about life, news, and politics to a population which never before had a way to be heard by the masses.

Sometimes, ripples grow into tsunamis, and a movement is born. Never underestimate the small things.

Judson Moore
Kyrgyzstan '11 – '13
JudsonLMoore.com
#whileyoung

SUMMER PROJECT IN QIJIANG, CHONGQING

There was a group of over 20 volunteers serving in the Chongqing municipality. We were spread all over the area, and some of us couldn't be reached by train but had to take hours-long bus rides. We lived from Chongqing City, to Wulong, to Wanzhou, and beyond. So many places, we could barely keep count.

By the beginning of our second year, we started to get the hang of our service and language got easier. Around our one-year anniversary as volunteers in China, it's mandatory to participate in what is called a Summer Project. It is a two-week long project that brings volunteers in each province together to educate Chinese English teachers on Western teaching methods. The volunteers will typically serve out their Summer Project at a school eligible for a PCV.

This summer project is planned just a few months in advance when the Peace Corps staff finally settles upon a location. Our China 20s group would be going to Qijiang, Chongqing, a small city one-hour outside of Chongqing City. This city was famous for a type of richly- colored painting known as "farmer printing" and their specialty cuisine, Beidu fish.

We found out our location and assignments in April and would be making our journey to Qijiang in June to start our Summer Project teaching exactly 300 teachers Western teaching methods. We had a few months to prepare teaching schedules, buddy up with our teaching partners, design lesson plans, and get ready for the heat and humidity promised by the city.

Since we like to volunteer, three of us volunteered to be teaching coordinators and logistics coordinators for the project. We started by taking a day trip to the site where we would spend two weeks teaching. What is considered a small city in China, is very large to us. Over 1.2 million people lived in Qijiang, nothing compared to the 11 million in Chongqing City.

Our first two days in Qijiang resulted in success, frustration, sleep deprivation, laughter, and smiles doused with unlimited pots of Beidu fish and Hot Pot.

81

We arrived in Qijiang after an hour drive to visit the city, dashing from one hotel to the other to see which one would be the best fit for our group. Amidst our journey, we also stopped at the local school to get a feel for the environment we would be working in. When we arrived to scope out the site, it was lunchtime. Lunch lasts for two hours in China, enough time to eat and take a nap. If they can't return to the dorms or live far from home, teachers and students will sleep at their desks after lunch. The school was silent in the busy city, and many desks were empty, but we were fortunate to cause a stir in a few classrooms once they noticed a handful of foreigners sneaking about their halls.

Knowledge of our presence caught on like wildfire and soon, the students began filing into the hallways to take pictures with us. We made their day.

The heartwarming day got us excited for the Summer Project. Before we knew it, the months leading up to Summer Project had gone by, and it was time to leave.

When the time came for Summer Project to begin, all volunteers met in the center of Chongqing City on a Sunday and piled into a bus with all of our suitcases to make the short trip. It was hot, everyone was sweating, and the sun blasted down on us like hellfire. We arrived in Qijiang once again after an hour drive, settled into the hotel, and then made a short trip to the school.

In China, it's not unusual to attend impromptu banquets and give impromptu speeches we most certainly weren't prepared for. This happened the first day we arrived when we were asked to visit each of our designated classrooms to introduce ourselves. It had already been a long day, and none of us were prepared, but nonetheless, we did it, awkwardly introduced ourselves, and then left to wind down for the evening. The next day was the first day of Summer Project.

The first week consisted of teaching all day, much like you would in the average classroom. 40 minutes of work and 10 minutes of rest. We divided the 300 teachers by the grade level they taught, Primary, Middle, and High School. We then divided each grade level into three groups. From there, three volunteer pairs per grade level rotated between the classrooms. As confusing as it was, it worked. We taught games and activities to the teachers and instructed them to build their own games and activities based on what they had learned. Most of the teachers attacked the lesson with enthusiasm I had never seen in my own Chinese classrooms.

As we taught our lessons throughout the week, we battled the teachers to close the windows and blast the AC in the 100+ degree weather, but they insisted on leaving them open to let in the "fresh," polluted air.

After a week, we were all tired and wanted nothing more than to sleep in. But in Peace Corps, you learn to get out and spend time with the people who host you. You spend the day doing fun things you would've missed if you were still sleeping.

Since the volunteers were separated by grade level, many of them split off into their groups to explore. With my group, we took a small adventure up and through towering hills near the city. They took us to a place called Nong Jia Le in the farmland areas. Nong Jia Le was beside a river, and a small cabin people could escape to. It was also a place you could catch fish with your bare hands and eat them for lunch.

Before we did our own fishing, we sat under a rectangular gazebo and feasted on warm watermelon and peanuts. We took a short walk upstream where we caught small crabs. We dipped our feet in the water and looked under rocks to find more crabs. Women stood under umbrellas as the sun beamed down, and we decided it was time to head back to start fishing.

Among the many occasions we couldn't be barefoot in China, other than our own homes, this was one occasion when we could take off our shoes and feel the earth between our toes. We gathered around a muddy pond filled with fish and tall weeds, took off our shoes, rolled up our pants, and climbed in. The young children followed us, linking their fingers in with ours.

We waded around in the muddy waters and watched an older man toss an open-ended wicker basket across the pond. We observed his techniques, waiting for air bubbles to burst at the surface. When air bubbles became visible, the man would throw the basket over bubbles then waded through the water toward the basket. He shoved his hands into the basket and slowly felt around for the fish. Once he claimed his prize, he pulled the fish from the waters and threw it into the bucket on the bank.

It took time to learn how to grab onto the fish. The faster you moved your hands, the less likely it was for you to catch a fish. The trick was to go slow when grabbing the fish. After we had caught much fish, we climbed out of the muddy pond, wiped down our legs, washed our hands, and went inside to have lunch. We ate the fish we caught and then headed back to the hotel to rest.

The next week went by quicker, but we were tired, and we were all ready to go home and relax during what was left of our summer vacation. We had built strong bonds with the generous people of Qijiang which made it a little harder to leave. The last few days of lessons were when our students started to feel more comfortable in the environment. They were more interactive, and they were more excited to learn. But as all things do, our time was ending.

On the last day, we presented the teachers who attended the project with certificates of completion, and some classes celebrated in their own ways with a talent show. Of course, we took grand pictures of all 300 teachers and all 30 volunteers out in front of the school and then made our way over to local restaurants to enjoy Beidu fish one last time.

Shortly after our lessons finished, we took countless group photos, hugged people goodbye, got the last few WeChat requests, and then packed up the bus to return to Chongqing City where we would resume our daily lives.

CLOSE OF SERVICE AND WHAT'S NEXT

THE DAY I CLOSED MY SERVICE was July 8th, 2016 and I was in Chengdu, Sichuan, at the Peace Corps headquarters. I climbed up and down four flights of stairs. I was getting signatures from members of the Peace Corps China staff, signatures that would approve my leaving the country of China, and completion of my service. Signature after signature, I felt nothing. No emotions, no sadness, no separation anxiety – nothing. By the time I reached my last signature, I hadn't even realized that this was the end. The man looked over my paperwork, checked for all the required signatures, and then signed off on the papers. He laid them down on the table and placed his hand out to shake mine. I took his hand to shake back.

"Thank you for your service." He said.

At that moment, it dawned on me, that I had completed two years I never thought possible. I would be leaving this home I created. I would be leaving my new-found family and friends. I did what I had set out to do. There was that emotion!

The sadness, the joy, the sense of accomplishment and the bittersweet feeling of something beautiful ending rushed over me. I left the office feeling everything I was holding back. How a simple phrase could make you feel so grateful and accomplished, well that's amazing. I cried on my way out.

After that, I spent one last evening with my host family and then headed back to Chongqing where I would collect my things and get ready to go home. I spent my last night in China in a hotel near the airport packing and repacking my bags, taking advantage of the bath that was in the hotel (bathtubs are not common in China) and had a relaxing last day before getting on a plane to go back to America.

If you've made it to your COS conference, you might be feeling extra emotional at this point. In spring, when trees are sprouting new leaves, flowers are blooming, and people are rolling up their thick comforters, you and the volunteers who have made it through service will be headed off to Peace Corps Headquarters to talk about your COS.

COS may have some mad feels for you, and even madder feels if you're especially emotional. You'll be missing your new Peace Corps family, leaving your new friends, saying goodbye to your students, and saying goodbye to your life. It's like you're starting a new life again. But hey, don't take this as being difficult. How beautiful it is to have things we love so much that it's hard to say goodbye.

When you get to COS, whether you have had a difficult experience or amazing experience, take out your journal and do this exercise. This will help you internalize all of the positive things you have experienced during your service, because, in the end, this is what will matter most.

Write a list of all of the things you love and are grateful for in your last two years of service. Include words like "I am grateful for…" or "I love…" or "I appreciate…" and try to stay away from negative tones like "I don't like…" or "I won't."

During COS, you'll have your last hurrah with volunteers you've grown close to. You'll take your final oral language test, talk about the ever-coming poop tubes, and sit through hours of training sessions instructing you on how you'll effectively complete your service. To be honest, COS conference is a lot like many of your other trainings, and if you're anything like our China 20s group, you'll stack the week with fun activities and tons of bonding!

Make sure you do this part, because you may regret not spending time with these people.

Our China 20s group spent the week hosting Zumba classes, Latin dance lessons, game nights, drinking nights at our favorite local bars, and Mexican dinners at China's famous Peter's Tex Mex. We ended our COS conference with a giant get together, dinner, and talent show we wouldn't forget. We handed out superlative awards for good laughs, put on talent show performances that tugged heartstrings, and made one last group memory together.

There's not much you will need to do to prepare for the COS conference, but there will be plenty to do after. That being said, there are a few things you can do before COS conference that is highly recommended.

STUDY LANGUAGE MORE
You will do an oral language test during COS conference, so it's best to practice as much as possible before you go in. That means, talking to people in your community as much as possible, taking lunch dates with your counterparts and asking them to critique you, or maybe it means sitting outside on a rock or in a chair at a Starbucks reviewing vocabulary. Whatever you do, study hard. Your final language assessment and language skill level could be useful when looking a great job in the future!

PREPARE FOR GRADUATE SCHOOL
Many in my group decided they wanted to go to school after they finished Peace Corps. Early on, they started studying for Graduate Record Examinations (GRE) and applying to schools. Even taking the GRE in-country where they could find it.

If you plan on going to school after your service, the best time to start getting ready and meeting all test requirements is right now. Don't forget, if this is what you're going for, you'll get sweet student aid along with it once you complete your service.

WORK ON RESUMES AND COVER LETTERS
This was part of our COS conference in China, and it was incredibly helpful. Come prepared. Bring your laptop or your tablet. Work on your resumes and cover letters before you head out for the conference. Even if it's a hard copy, you'll be able to sit down with someone who knows how to write resumes and cover letters, and they can help you make it stronger.

When the time comes to start applying for jobs, you will be more than prepared.

START APPLYING FOR JOBS AND INTERNSHIPS

It might seem like a stretch, but I started checking out the job pool as many as six months before leaving China. I could see what was out there in relation to what I wanted to do next. The hiring process can be lengthy for some people, taking anywhere from 2 – 4 weeks to 2 – 3 months to find a job. It's best to start early. If you're lucky, you could find a job or internship by the time you leave your country! Try setting up job interviews via Skype to secure a spot. You'll also be getting your Non-Competitive Eligibility (NCE) letter which affords your resume priority when applying for government jobs. Attach it to your resume and your applications will be placed above other candidates. If you can, ask for your NCE early to help speed up your job search.

START PACKING:

I know it seems early, but this is a good practice. When you start packing, you'll fill your bags with things you think are essential to take home with you. And believe me, you will want to take as much as possible. I started a few months out, that way I could unpack and repack several times before I went home. We as humans have tendencies to change our minds about things.

REMEMBER YOUR STUDENT LOANS

After Peace Corps, your loans will be reinstated. But don't worry, chances are they won't start kicking in for several months after you return. Either way, contact your loan providers to get an idea of when you will start paying on loans. If you know ahead of time, you can add it to your calendar, and be prepared when the time comes.

BRINGING THE JOURNEY HOME

I'VE BEEN stateside now for nearly 27 months, which is slightly longer than the 26-month-long period in which I served in the Peace Corps. Once I got over the reverse- culture shock and went through my readjustment period, I began the seemingly never-ending process of reflecting upon and reevaluating my time abroad. Let's just say I've analyzed every aspect of my time in Liberia, West Africa and as a Peace Corps Volunteer.

Being in Liberia was definitely "not easy-oh". I was a Secondary Education Volunteer, teaching middle school general science and high school biology in a small, rural village with no laboratory, no library or textbooks, and no modern living amenities such as running water and electricity. On top of this, constantly adjusting oneself to be as culturally-appropriate as possible at all times and striving to be a successful teacher, role model, and representative (of so many entities) was exhausting. It was the most emotionally and psychologically trying period of my life. With that said, I wouldn't change it for anything. People often ask me, "Overall, did you enjoy your time over there? Would you go back?"

Without hesitation, I answer, "Absolutely," every time.

I like to think I helped the people I interacted with, even if just a little bit.

90

While my former students may not remember the function of mitochondria in a cell or the formula for calculating the force of an object given the mass and acceleration, I can confidently say they'll remember some of the "life lessons" I taught them. One that easily comes to mind is why it's important not to spy (cheat) in class. But what I've come to realize is that Liberians helped me more than I helped them.

Liberia made me better; it made me stronger. Liberia taught me to have thick skin and to let other's negative words roll off my back. It taught me how to read people, to foresee situations that could have disadvantageous results towards myself and my friends and steer clear. It opened my naïve eyes to the often not-so-pretty way the world of developmental aid operates, but it also taught me to take many things with a grain of salt. Liberians exude self- confidence, and that definitely rubbed off on me too; I never felt more comfortable in my own skin than during my service.

Overall, being a Peace Corps Volunteer in Liberia taught me to be flexible, resourceful, patient, and to have a sense of humor at all times.
And, most importantly of all, Liberia taught me to love.

I came to love my community, my students, and some of my neighbors...even "mother f-ing Momo," the 2-year-old neighbor boy with his daily hysterical temper tantrums. I came to love wholeheartedly the way Liberians value their sense of community, the way they care for one another, and the way they love their culture and their country. And I came to love their culture and their country, too.

Mama Liberia also helped me learn to and begin to love myself.

Who knows what the future holds. I don't think I'll ever live in Liberia again, but I do plan on visiting in the next couple of years and hope to continue to keep in touch with those whom I care about over there. Liberia will always be a second home to me in my heart and mind. All I know is that I'll be better prepared for whatever comes my way because of my time in the Peace Corps, and for that, I am grateful.

Danielle J. Zemmel
Liberia '12 – '14

If that didn't make you cry, I don't know what will. Danielle's story is a great example of what most volunteers will feel upon returning home from 27 months of a very different life. In her story, you can understand just how much you are changed for the better, and how in even the most difficult situations you learn the power of love. Of the many of us that have started

Peace Corps, and finished it, we can usually agree on one thing: it changed our lives.

After it has changed our lives, it goes on to change our futures as well. It changes how we view the world, how we see its people, how we value people and things, and it helps us determine what the next best step is.

Before we finish up this chapter, let's do one last exercise.

- How will you verbalize your experience to your family, friends, and community?
- What things will you do to promote the journey of Peace Corps after service?

Many people will return home, close the book on the Peace Corps life and never speak of it again. Some will return home and find themselves back in the Peace Corps office to continue the mission of positive cross-cultural relations. Others may have decided two years abroad wasn't enough, so they decide to continue the travels.

For many of us, we returned home, found new jobs, new homes, new cars, and started a new life while the good times of Peace Corps still linger. Stories of Peace Corps will drop lightly into conversations with new people and old friends.

Some may be interested, some may not. People back home may not be able to relate, and that is certainly okay. That's why keeping a journal is so important! It allows you to go back and relive the good parts, laugh at the funny parts, and let go of the worst parts. You know your journey, and you don't have to explain it to anyone.

When I arrived home, I was a completely different person in a lot of ways similar to Danielle's experience. My father told me I was so much quieter and listened so much more intently that it was "disarming." Not necessarily a bad thing, just a testament to how I had changed. In addition to adjusting to culture again, it was time to move forward, let go of what was, and find the next adventure. I searched for two months before I found the job that would take me to that next phase of my life.

It turned out Peace Corps was what gave me the jumpstart to my current career in the advertising world. But what lingered with me more and more each day, were the number of potential volunteers out there struggling to decide whether Peace Corps is even the right choice. I wanted more than anything to encourage them that joining was a good decision, and a brave one. Many have thanked me for the stories I've shared on TravelBranyik.com because it's helped them make that final decision to join.

Knowing what I know now, I want to help those out there searching for the next adventure or experience. I suspect this is one of the reasons why we have so many fantastic Peace Corps Recruiters still working for the three goals each year.

This is my last bit of advice for everyone as you get ready to leave your home, wherever you are.

THIRD GOALING IT
Peace Corps third goal, if you've already forgotten, is "To help promote a better understanding of other peoples on the part of Americans." This goal asks you to bring home the culture, the understanding, and the journey and share it.

Share it with your family and friends by cooking them an authentic dinner, visiting recruitment seminars at local universities, sharing your stories on a blog. Whatever it is, your goal is to share it, to get people excited, to let them know how amazing your last few years have been. Be excited to share! Do it when you're ready and when there reverse culture shock wears off.

READJUSTMENT ALLOWANCE
This bad boy has so much potential and was implemented to give volunteers a nice financial cushion as they integrate back into American culture. If you don't find a job immediately, this is meant to assist you as you look for one. Your Readjustment Allowance is distributed in parts, one-half before leaving and the other half a few days after you COS. You will not get the whole amount at once or earlier than expected. You must finish your service before you walk off with wads of cash, and it won't actually be wads of cash.

For those of you finishing service, I want to tell you something. From the time you step off the plane onto American soil, remember, YOU ARE HUMAN. Although it may seem like you're alienated, you're not. You're just very awake to the world now, and that is what makes you different.

You may experience reverse culture shock. You may stand in the shampoo aisle for 45 minutes looking at all the choices. You may gain 25 pounds of the weight you lost because of delicious American foods. You may wonder how you can even live in America. You may be overwhelmed by the copious amounts of running water you have. You may feel that your life is boring because you aren't adventuring anymore. Whatever your worry, take it in strides. Rely on the people who love you. Ask them for help. People who love you will be patient, just like your host families were with you. And, you can always talk to your journal.

You will emerge a completely different, even more wonderful person than the one you were before. You'll have more than just rose-colored glasses. You will have an entire rainbow collection to see things in a whole new light. You will understand people in ways you never could before. They will help you understand yourself, find your next journey, or leave you with lingering questions about what more you can do for yourself.

You may be sad for the end of your service. But remember to be excited about the next phase of your life. Know that all the memories you have created in that precious two-year span will always be with you. If no one cares about your experience or loses interest in your stories because they can't relate, let it go, you know the meaning of your service. The ones who love you will understand the journey, pay attention, and be supportive. And if you feel like you need a hand reintegrating to your home country, rely on the Peace Corps family. They will stay with you forever.

What you experienced in your service was beautiful, perfect, and just as it should've been. Regret nothing and embrace all of what you experienced. Even the worst things can be catalysts for incredible self-growth.

When you come home, you have the opportunity to inspire others to see the world. Encourage them to join the Peace Corps. Share your valuable stories. Whether in Washington D.C., Denver, Boston, Seattle, San Francisco, Albuquerque, or Atlanta, Peace Corps is always encouraging the volunteer family to come together and celebrate the bonds created during their service.

You'll have opportunities to impart your wisdom to the world to make a positive impact. When you do, embrace the opportunity and take advantage of that situation. All you have done was magnificent, and you should pat yourself on the back because you did it!

So, what will happen after you return from Peace Corps? To be honest, it depends... On you.

HELPFUL RESOURCES

MUCH OF OUR PEACE CORPS successes have been achieved through the beautiful acts of teamwork. For this reason, I reference the many great authors who have come out of Peace Corps and contributed their stories and advice over the years to both share their story and inspire people to join in the experience. Below are those great authors.

I encourage you to read their novels and guides as well to gain as many different perspectives as possible.

BOOKS

"The Peace Corps Volunteer's Handbook: A Personal Field Guide to Making the Most of Your Peace Corps Experience"
by Travis Hellstrom

"The Insider's Guide to Peace Corps: What to Know Before You Go"
by Dillon Banerjee

"Rivertown"
By Peter Hessler

"Living Poor: A Peace Corps Chronicle"
By Moritz Thomsen

"Living Poor: A Peace Corps Chronicle"
by Moritz Thomsen

"Kosher Chinese"
by Michael Levy

"When the World Calls"
by Stanley Meisler

"One Hand Does Not Catch a Buffalo: 50 Years of Amazing Peace Corps Stories"
by Aaron Barlow

WEBSITES & BLOGS

Peace Corps
The official website for Peace Corps is loaded with all the information you need to know about joining Peace Corps. Talk with a Recruiter, attend an event, and read stories from volunteers.
www.PeaceCorps.gov

Kelly Branyik
My personal blog highlights my service as a volunteer in Peace Corps China and my efforts as a traveler and a writer. It is loaded with advice and stories that encourage and inspire the journey.
www.TravelBranyik.com

Judson L. Moore
Judson is a former Peace Corps Volunteer who shares very detailed and entertaining stories about travel and about Peace Corps. You can find many amazing stories on his website.
www.JudsonLMoore.com

National Peace Corps Association
Your resource for connecting with other volunteers around the globe, even after your service has been completed.
www.PeaceCorpsConnect.org

Blog It Home
Blog It Home Began in 2013 and since then has hosted blogs from over 1,000 volunteers in service. Their blog has reached over 1 million people and appears as the number Peace Corps blog on the search results.
www.PeaceCorps.gov/returned-volunteers/awards/blog-it-hom

ABOUT THE AUTHOR

KELLY KATHLEEN BRANYIK is a graduate of Colorado State University in Pueblo, Colorado. Her passion for writing began when she was a third grader in Florence, Colorado and it has been driving her ever since.

Kelly stills talks about the Peace Corps journey and experience and enjoys writing to inspire others to do and accomplish great things. She pilots her online blog sharing her stories, and the experiences of others to motivate people to see more of the world.

Kelly was the first and the last volunteer at her school in China; Chongqing Vocational Tourism School.

"It Depends: A Guide to Peace Corps" is Kelly's first book, but certainly not her last one. You can learn more about her Peace Corps adventures online at TravelBranyik.com.

This hand guide is an ongoing project and will have updated editions in the future. If you felt this book was missing information you were hoping to see, or you are a Peace Corps Volunteer who wants share your stories in the next edition, please send your recommendations and stories to Kelly @travelbranyik.com.

You can follow Kelly on Facebook, Instagram, and Twitter at @TravelBranyik for more advice on Peace Corps and her travels.

Made in the USA
Columbia, SC
08 January 2019